Music Legends

40 inspiring icons

Hervé Guilleminot & Jérôme Masi

WIDE EYED EDITIONS

Rock Around the Decades

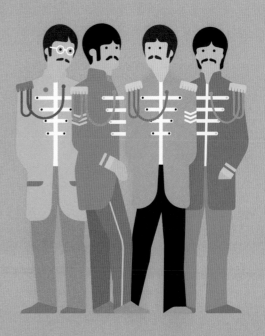

Elvis Presley recorded "That's All Right (Mama)" in 1954, in a small studio in Memphis in the South of the United States. It was a mix of rhythm and blues, which had African American origins, and of country music, which had its roots in European folk music. This unique sound sparked the rock revolution, which quickly spread to the United Kingdom—and the rest of the world.

The Beatles, the Rolling Stones and later the Who took the next steps in the evolution of so-called 'popular music' – or pop, for short – and provided a soundtrack to the fast-changing society of the 1960s. Since then, rock and pop music has continually reinvented itself, absorbing new sounds and responding to the issues faced by each new generation to produce a kaleidoscope of different kinds of music.

From the hypnotic, psychedelic rock of 1960s hippies, to the protest songs and folk music of the 1960s and 1970s, to hard rock – with its aggressive vocals and distorted sounds – to the laid-back Caribbean beat of reggae, to the eccentricity and sparkle of glam rock in the 1970s, to the bitter urban brutality of punk rock in the 1980s, to the steely atmosphere of the new wave, to the hip-hop music that came out of the streets of the U.S. and came to define the 1990s (not forgetting everything that happened in between), each year, wave upon wave of musicians have woven new strands into the fabric of pop music, right up to this day, and inspired new sounds, as well as the revival of old sounds, as new generations of artists are influenced by their forebears. Want to know more? Here are 40 famous artists and groups who have helped to write the fabulous history of rock.

Contents

21

SEX PISTOLS

22

THE CLASH

23

U2

24

THE POLICE

25

THE CURE

26

DEPECHE MODE

27

NEW ORDER

28

THE SMITHS

29

MADONNA

30

RED HOT
CHILI PEPPERS

31

N.W.A

32

PIXIES

33

NIRVANA

34

BLUR

35

RADIOHEAD

36

WU-TANG CLAN

37

DAFT PUNK

38

THE WHITE STRIPES

39

BEYONCÉ

40

ARCADE FIRE

Elvis Presley

With the face of an angel, and devilish swivelling hips, Mississippi-born Elvis Presley's great popularity as a live performer was increased by his chart-busting records, television appearances and Hollywood films. A musical superstar from the beginnings of rock 'n' roll in 1954, he stole the limelight from 'the Rat Pack' – the world-famous Las Vegas crooners – though in turn he himself was made to look outdated by British pop in the 1960s. Nevertheless, he remains a global icon and the legend of 'the King' lives on!

CULTURAL MIX

From the outset, Elvis fused hillbilly and country music with rhythm and blues to create a new sound, which came to be known as 'rockabilly'. With his look, his style, his music, and his way of life, he embodied rock 'n' roll.

5 DATES

1935
Born in Tupelo (Mississippi)

1954
Began at Studio Sun (Memphis)

1958-1960
Drafted into the U.S. Army

1968
Live *Comeback Special* on American television

1977
Died in Memphis (Tennessee)

CONCERT

After a seven-year hiatus, in 1968, NBC broadcast the *Comeback Special*. Dressed in a black leather suit featuring an upturned collar (which became a signature look), he was a massive hit.

STAGE AND SCREEN

People often forget that although Elvis was the 'father of rock', he was also an actor (he was in 31 films) and often performed onstage. He put on more than 1,100 concerts in the United States, half of which were in Las Vegas.

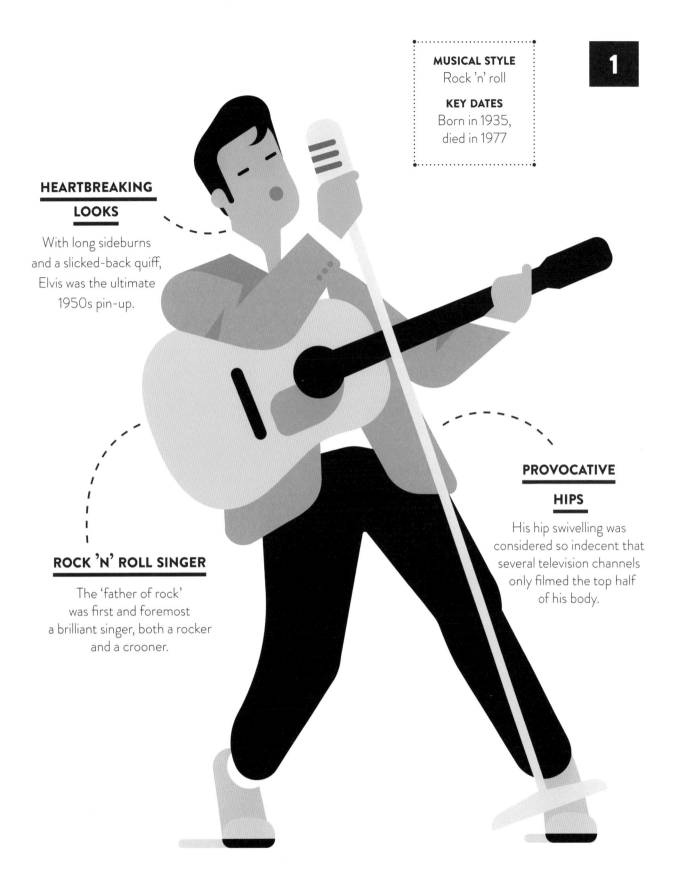

MUSICAL STYLE
Rock 'n' roll

KEY DATES
Born in 1935,
died in 1977

HEARTBREAKING

LOOKS

With long sideburns
and a slicked-back quiff,
Elvis was the ultimate
1950s pin-up.

PROVOCATIVE

HIPS

His hip swivelling was
considered so indecent that
several television channels
only filmed the top half
of his body.

ROCK 'N' ROLL SINGER

The 'father of rock'
was first and foremost
a brilliant singer, both a rocker
and a crooner.

The King

Bob Dylan

In 1961, Bob Dylan arrived in Greenwich Village, a bohemian neighbourhood in New York, and soon became a leading light of the American folk music revival. The counterculture messages of 'Blowin' in the Wind' and 'The Times They Are a-Changin'' saw the songs adopted by the civil rights movement and anti-war movement. But then, defying his fans, the ever-evolving Dylan left behind folk songs to incorporate pop and rock influences, releasing the revolutionary 'Like a Rolling Stone' in 1965, which cemented him as a major global artist.

NOBEL PRIZE

In 2016, Dylan became the first songwriter to be awarded the Nobel Prize in Literature 'for having created new poetic expressions within the great American song tradition'. Never afraid to defy convention, he waited two weeks before acknowledging the accolade.

SELECTED DISCOGRAPHY

1964
The Times They Are a-Changin''

1966
Blonde on Blonde

1969
Nashville Skyline

1975
Blood on the Tracks

2006
Modern Times

INFLUENCE

At the beginning of his songwriting career, Dylan was influenced by the great protest songwriter Woody Guthrie and blues singer Lead Belly.

NEVER ENDING TOUR

In 1988, the Never Ending Tour gave Dylan an opportunity to return to his best-known songs, improvising onstage. The musicians would change numbers every evening and perform the songs differently from one night to the next.

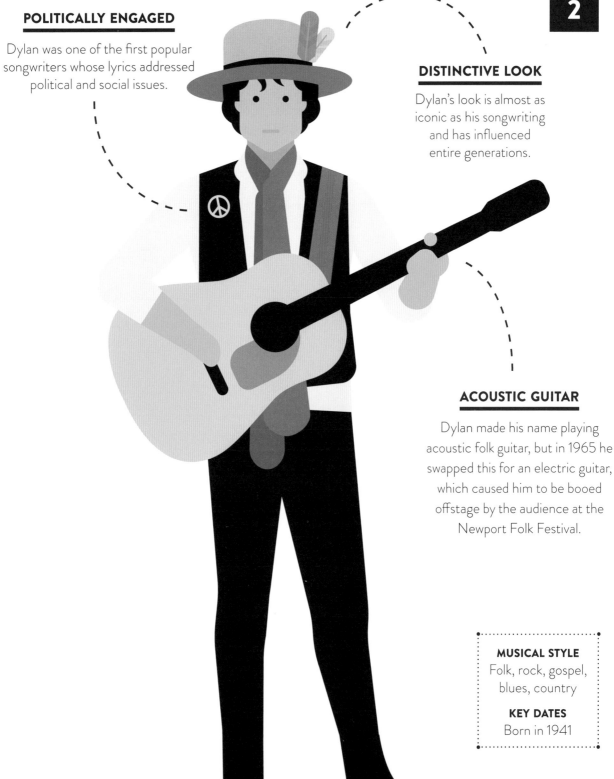

POLITICALLY ENGAGED

Dylan was one of the first popular songwriters whose lyrics addressed political and social issues.

DISTINCTIVE LOOK

Dylan's look is almost as iconic as his songwriting and has influenced entire generations.

ACOUSTIC GUITAR

Dylan made his name playing acoustic folk guitar, but in 1965 he swapped this for an electric guitar, which caused him to be booed offstage by the audience at the Newport Folk Festival.

MUSICAL STYLE
Folk, rock, gospel, blues, country

KEY DATES
Born in 1941

Voice of a generation

The Beatles

Embodying the sound of the Merseybeat in 1960s Liverpool, 'Beatlemania' took the world by storm and in 1964 they conquered the U.S., in the so-called 'British Invasion'.

If music history had to choose its most important pop group, it would be the Beatles. Why? Because no other group has dominated its generation to such an extent. The 'Fab Four' pioneered new styles of music, but their influence was felt far beyond this realm, as they trailblazed new ideas in film, fashion and political activism, which collectively came to encapsulate 1960s counterculture. Creating such hysteria among their fans that their music couldn't be heard above the screaming at their concerts, today they remain the best-selling band in history.

RECIPE FOR SUCCESS

Behind the scenes, the Beatles were managed and supported by two icons of pop music: George Martin, their producer, and Brian Epstein, their manager. Together, they anticipated and dominated every trend, from pop, to psychedelic music and rock.

SELECTED DISCOGRAPHY

1964
A Hard Day's Night

1966
Revolver

1967
Sgt. Pepper's Lonely Hearts Club Band

1968
The White Album

1969
Abbey Road

1970
Let It Be

MAJOR ALBUM

'Yesterday', which appeared on their 1965 album *Help!*, is the most-covered song in the world: as it stands, there are 3,000 versions!

CONCEPT ALBUM

In 1966, the Beatles got tired of giving concerts and chose to stay in the studio to produce albums. They moved beyond the classic 45s to make new and conceptual albums, of which *Sgt. Pepper* (1967) is the perfect example.

MUSICAL STYLE
Pop-rock

KEY DATES
Founded in 1962,
broke up in 1970

LENNON/MCCARTNEY
This unrivalled singer-songwriting
partnership saw John and Paul
write nearly 200 songs together!

**SGT. PEPPER'S LONELY
HEARTS CLUB BAND**
These psychedelic costumes
appeared on the album cover
of pop music's masterpiece.

MEMBERS

John Lennon,
Ringo Starr,
Paul McCartney,
and George
Harrison

The Fab Four

The Rolling Stones

London, 1962, played backdrop to the formation of the Rolling Stones – a band that would go on to rock the world for more than 50 years. The band's five turbulent decades have seen dramatic ups and downs, including changes in line-up, the tragic death of the band's founding member Brian Jones, and countless legal and personal problems. Nevertheless, fans and critics alike have shown their committed support for the 'World's Greatest Rock and Roll Band', and today the band has sold more than 200 million albums worldwide.

CONCERT

Shortly after Brian Jones's death, a concertgoer was brutally killed at the Altamont Free Concert (hosted by the Stones), making 1969 one of the toughest years in the band's history.

SELECTED DISCOGRAPHY

1969
Let It Bleed

1971
Sticky Fingers

1972
Exile on Main St.

1974
It's Only Rock 'n' Roll

CHANGING LINE-UP

The original (constant) line-up, featuring Mick Jagger, Keith Richards, Brian Jones, Bill Wyman, Charlie Watts and Ian Stewart, changed when Jones left the group just a month before his death in 1969. Mick Taylor took his place, and Ron Wood took his in turn, in 1975.

STICKY FINGERS

The iconic Rolling Stones' logo, a pair of red lips and lapping tongue, was inspired by Mick Jagger's mouth. It was created in 1970 by John Pasche, an art student at the Royal College of Art in London and first appeared on the Stones' album *Sticky Fingers*, in 1971.

INFLUENCE

One of their sources of inspiration was blues music, with the Stones taking their name from 'Rollin' Stone', a song by Muddy Waters.

BAD BOYS

With leather jackets, big hair and bare chests, the Stones offered the perfect 'bad boy' alternative to the Beatles.

BRIAN JONES

The original founder's increasingly turbulent lifestyle led to him being fired by the band in 1969.

LONG HISTORY

Mick Jagger and Keith Richards, who wrote most of the Stones' hits, first met at primary school.

MUSICAL STYLE
Blues rock, rhythm 'n' blues, psychedelic rock

KEY DATES
Founded in 1962

The Stones

The Who

Originally billed as the Detours, then the High Numbers, then finally the Who, this London-based band put on incredible live shows for four decades, and helped to write one of the most intense chapters of rock history. The singers of 'My Generation' had a lasting effect on rock music for generations of artists to come: their musical journey, which began with their mod roots and later encompassed psychedelic music and rock operas, saw them smash everything in their path: drumsets, guitars... even their hotel rooms!

BRITISH INVASION

From the 1960s, The Who were part of the 'British Invasion', a term used in the United States to describe the wave of British groups (the Beatles, the Rolling Stones, the Animals, the Kinks) that took over the American charts and stages.

Over

100

million albums sold in the world!

CSI

Each series of the TV show *CSI* has a song by the group as its theme tune: 'Won't Get Fooled Again' for *Miami*, 'Who Are You' for *Las Vegas*, 'Baba O'Riley' for *Manhattan* and 'I Can See for Miles' for *Cyber*. A nice bit of product placement for the band!

MAJOR ALBUM

A recording of their concert on 14 February 1970 at Leeds University resulted in the now-legendary live album *Live at Leeds*.

5 DATES

1965
My Generation

1969
Rock opera
Tommy

1973
Quadrophenia

1978
Death of Keith Moon

2002
Death of John Entwistle

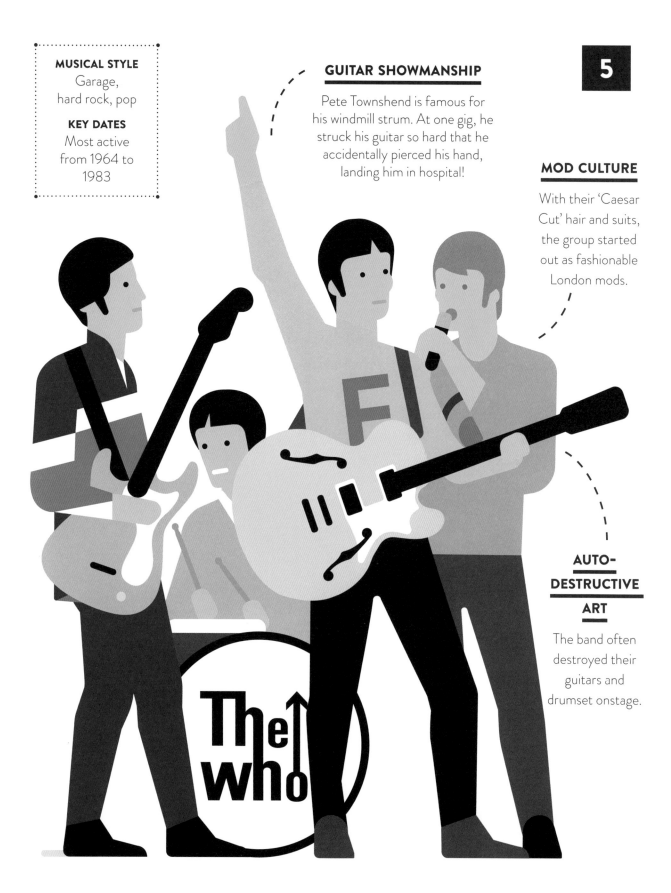

MUSICAL STYLE
Garage, hard rock, pop

KEY DATES
Most active from 1964 to 1983

GUITAR SHOWMANSHIP
Pete Townshend is famous for his windmill strum. At one gig, he struck his guitar so hard that he accidentally pierced his hand, landing him in hospital!

MOD CULTURE
With their 'Caesar Cut' hair and suits, the group started out as fashionable London mods.

AUTO-DESTRUCTIVE ART
The band often destroyed their guitars and drumset onstage.

The High Numbers

The Doors

With a tormented blues-rock style that fed into the psychedelic scene, the Doors, who hailed from Los Angeles, developed a literary, poetic style of rock with serious themes that were rarely attempted in pop music. Yet somehow, thanks to the charisma and wildness of vocalist Jim Morrison, they managed to carry it off. But the more interest there was in the group, the more Morrison descended into self-doubt and self-destruction. Finally disbanding in 1973, their albums pay testament to a uniquely disjointed and tortured music career.

More than

100

million albums sold in the world!

MAJOR ALBUM

If music history had to pick just one of their albums, it would be *The Doors*, from 1967. It has everything, and shows their various influences, richness... and madness.

JIM MORRISON

During 1967, when the Doors began to break out, Jim Morrison seemed reluctant to embrace fame, and his self-destructive urges became even stronger. Despite his early death in 1971, he remains one of the best-remembered frontmen of all time.

LITERARY ORIGINS

Befitting of their poetic style of rock, their name came from Aldous Huxley's book *The Doors of Perception*, which in turn harked back to a William Blake quote: "If the doors of perception were cleansed, everything would appear to man as it is, infinite".

5 DATES

January 1967
The Doors

September 1967
Strange Days

April 1971
L.A. Woman

3 July 1971
Death of Jim Morrison

20 May 2013
Death of Ray Manzarek

MUSICAL STYLE
Acid rock, psychedelic music

KEY DATES
Group founded in 1965, and split up in 1973

JIM MORRISON — THE ICON

Poet, singer, performer... Morrison ensured his legendary status by becoming the first rock artist ever to be arrested onstage.

BASSLINE

Ray Manzarek's Fender Rhodes replaced the more usual bass guitar in the band's line-up.

CATCHING FIRE

After years in obscurity, their single 'Light My Fire' took them to #1 on the U.S. charts.

The Doors of Perception

The Velvet Underground

The minimalist, dissonant music of the Velvet Underground offered a completely different sound to the psychedelic pop of the 1960s. Formed in New York City by singer-songwriter Lou Reed, the band's gritty subject matter and avant-garde sound brought them to the attention of pop art icon Andy Warhol, whose peelable banana sticker featured on the front cover of their 1967 album, *The Velvet Underground and Nico*. Although the album sold very few copies at the time, it is now widely recognised as one of the greatest albums of all time.

5 DATES

1967
The Velvet Underground & Nico

1968
White Light/ White Heat

1970
Loaded

1993
Group reunites

2013
Death of Lou Reed

NAMESAKE

After earlier incarnations as the Warlocks, then the Falling Spikes, the group finally settled on the name the Velvet Underground in 1965, after a friend of the group chanced upon a copy of the book by Michael Leigh in the street.

VIEW OF a PRO

Recognising the significance of *The Velvet Underground and Nico*, Brian Eno said that despite the poor sales of just 30,000 copies in five years, "everyone who bought one of those 30,000 copies started a band"!

MAJOR ALBUM

Recorded live, *Olympia MCMXCIII* rekindled interest in the group in 1993.

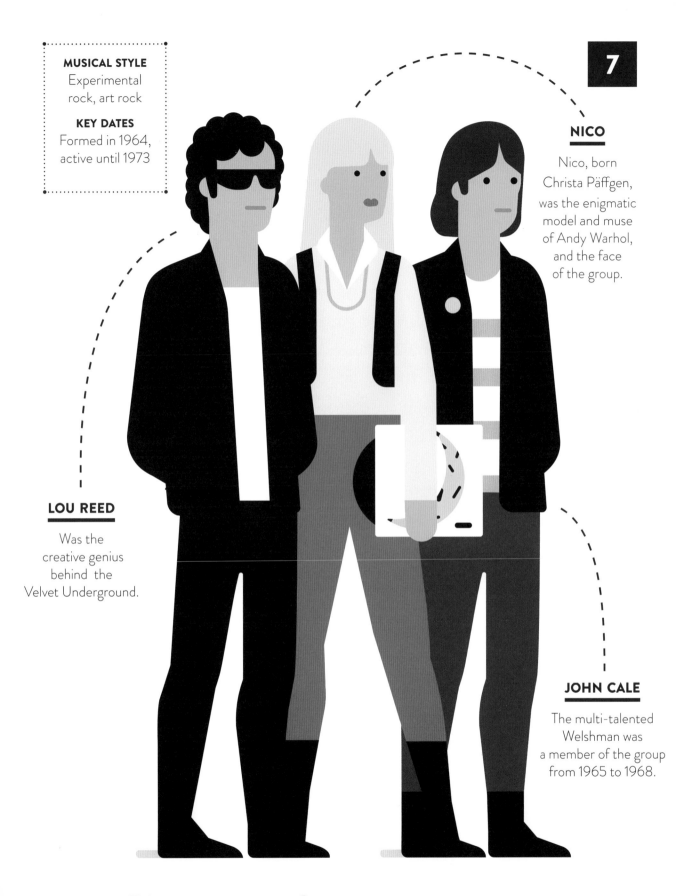

MUSICAL STYLE
Experimental rock, art rock

KEY DATES
Formed in 1964, active until 1973

NICO

Nico, born Christa Päffgen, was the enigmatic model and muse of Andy Warhol, and the face of the group.

LOU REED

Was the creative genius behind the Velvet Underground.

JOHN CALE

The multi-talented Welshman was a member of the group from 1965 to 1968.

The sound of the underground

Pink Floyd

EXPERIMENTATION

In *Meddle*, a cult album which came out in 1971, Pink Floyd experimented and explored using layers of ambient music.

Emerging from London's underground scene towards the end of the 1960s, Pink Floyd experimented with several different styles of music, from psychedelic pop, through progressive rock, to synth rock and pop-rock. Ever-evolving, the group became renowned for their thought-provoking lyrics, exploration of new sounds, and epic live shows, which made use of extravagant light shows, bespoke animations, and even large inflatable puppets! Always ahead of the times, many of their songs have since become timeless classics.

OUT OF THIS WORLD

With *The Dark Side of the Moon*, the band pioneered new technology, using multitrack recording, tape loops and analogue synthesizers to produce a new sonic experience for their listeners. It became their best-selling album with 45 million copies sold.

5 DATES

1965
Set up in London

1966-1968
Psychedelic beginnings with Syd Barrett

1973
Dark Side of the Moon

1979
The Wall

2006 and 2008
Syd Barrett and Richard Wright die

CONCERT

The band toured around the world, taking their amazing shows to grand locations like Versailles, Venice and Pompei – a long way from the underground clubs where they started out.

A DARK VISION

Roger Waters's lyrics, which dwelled on political oppression, war, alienation and mental illness, saw him dubbed 'the gloomiest man in rock'. Nevertheless, they spoke to a disillusioned generation of fans, and inspired new groups for decades to come.

MUSICAL STYLE
Psychedelic music, ambient pop, art rock

KEY DATES
Active from 1965 to 1994

DAVID GILMOUR AND ROGER WATERS

Between them, these songwriters created most of Pink Floyd's hits.

DARK SIDE OF THE MOON

The iconic prism design was created after the band requested a cover that was 'smarter, neater – more classy' than their earlier albums.

EMS VSC3

This synthesizer helped create the *Dark Side of the Moon*'s trippy sound!

Psychedelic

Jimi Hendrix

The uncontested master of the guitar, the list of artists inspired by Jimi Hendrix's playing is long. But the career of this self-taught guitarist was brief: four years in the spotlight, a handful of albums, and a string of memorable concerts were cut short by his tragic, untimely death at the age of just 27. Charismatic, curious, poetic, and technically accomplished, he was an incredible improvisor, producing music that embodied the cultural melting pot of 1960s America, combining blues, psychadelic rock and R&B.

CONCERT

In 1969, Hendrix closed Woodstock, after staying awake for three days. He gave an electrifying rendition of 'The Star-Spangled Banner', played 'Hey Joe' as the encore, then collapsed offstage, exhausted.

Hendrix will be forever associated with his favourite guitar: a Fender Stratocaster.

BOTH-HANDED

Hendrix was a natural left-hander, and usually played a restrung right-hand guitar upside down, but he could also play right-handed: an incredible feat!

SPECIAL FX

Hendrix pushed the electric guitar to new limits, making sounds impossible to recreate on an acoustic guitar. He experimented with amplification, feedback, wah-wah pedals, vibrato, overdriven amplifiers and stereophonic phasing to create his own unique sound.

MAKING HIS MARK

Hendrix became a star the world over and travelled to London. There, he stayed in a house next door to composer George Handel's former home. After his death, a blue plaque was put up to commemorate his time there, the first time a pop star was given this accolade.

SELECTED DISCOGRAPHY

May 1967
Are You Experienced

December 1967
Axis: Bold as Love

1968
Electric Ladyland

1970
Band of Gypsys

1999
Live at Woodstock (1969 concert)

ON FIRE

Not to be outdone by the Who, Hendrix set fire to his guitar at the 1967 Monterey Pop Festival.

STYLE ICON

Resplendent in his bandana, flairs and open-neck shirts, the handsome Hendrix's flamboyant style won him a legion of admirers.

DOUBLY TALENTED

Naturally left-handed, Hendrix could play – and write – right-handed, because his father thought left-handedness was a sign of the devil!

MUSICAL STYLE
Blues, psychedelic rock, hard rock, R&B

KEY DATES
Born in 1942
Died in 1970

The legendary Jimi

Genesis

Pioneers of progressive rock with complex rhythms and harmonies, British rock group Genesis was formed by five Charterhouse School students. The band went on to have two distinct periods: the first with the theatrical Peter Gabriel as frontman, when the band were famed for Gabriel's outrageous make-up, ostentatious costumes, and unusual singing; the second saw Phil Collins, the band's drummer, succeed Gabriel as lead singer, marking the beginning of a more commercial period for the band.

SILVER SPOON

Against a grim backdrop of economic uncertainty, the band's style of progressive rock, combined with their private school backgrounds, led them to be criticised for 'taking rock away from the working classes'. Nevertheless, their music stood the test of time.

SELECTED DISCOGRAPHY

1970
Trespass

1971
Nursery Cryme

1972
Foxtrot

1973
Selling England by the Pound

1974
The Lamb Lies Down on Broadway

MAJOR ALBUM

Foxtrot (1972) was the group's fourth album. One of the tracks, 'Supper's Ready', lasts twenty-three minutes – a masterpiece of progressive rock.

SECOND LIFE

Life wasn't over for former members after leaving Genesis. Gabriel went on to enjoy a solo career and co-found world music festival WOMAD; Collins also went solo and turned to acting; while Rutherford founded the group Mike + the Mechanics.

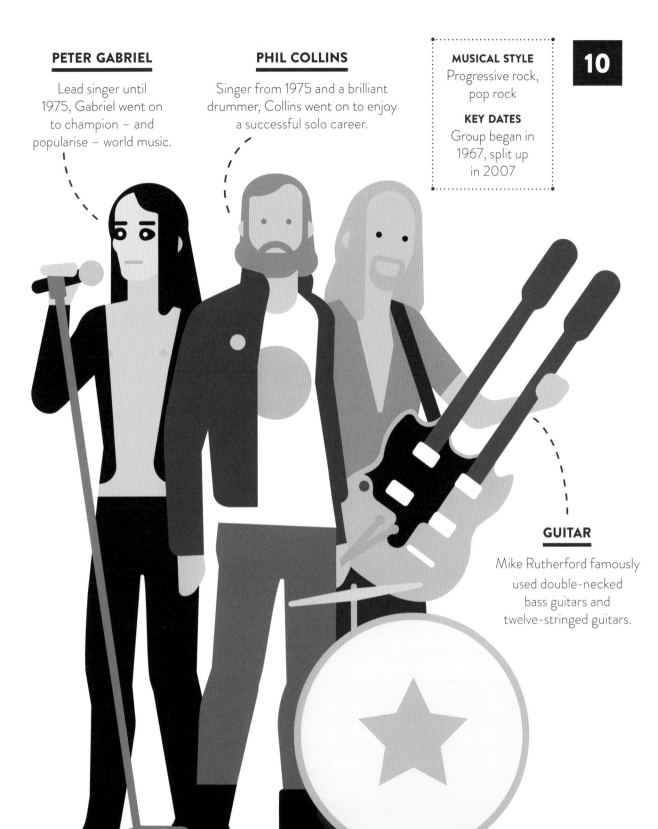

PETER GABRIEL

Lead singer until 1975, Gabriel went on to champion – and popularise – world music.

PHIL COLLINS

Singer from 1975 and a brilliant drummer, Collins went on to enjoy a successful solo career.

MUSICAL STYLE
Progressive rock, pop rock

KEY DATES
Group began in 1967, split up in 2007

10

GUITAR

Mike Rutherford famously used double-necked bass guitars and twelve-stringed guitars.

Ambassadors of prog rock

Neil Young

After a career spanning fifty years, Canadian singer-songwriter Neil Young remains as committed to his music as ever. Alongside numerous collaborations throughout his career, including Buffalo Springfield, Crazy Horse, Pearl Jam, and Crosby, Stills & Nash, to name but a few, Young has also proved himself as a solo artist, releasing album after iconic album. His authentic voice and unflinching lyrics still command the respect of younger fans today – time has taken nothing away from this valiant rock soldier.

BACKGROUND

Originally hailing from Toronto, Canada, Young moved to the U.S. in 1965, and never returned from his new home in California... Nevertheless, he kept his Canadian passport!

36
albums recorded so far!

SELECTED DISCOGRAPHY

1970
After the Gold Rush

1972
Harvest

1991
Arc/Weld

1992
Harvest Moon

1994
Sleep with Angels

DIVERSE STYLES

Young's musical style is impossible to define – he's tried everything! From folk and country in his youth, to rockabilly, electronic music, jazz, grunge, blues and synth later in his career – he's a musical chameleon with an impressive ability to change.

MAN ON A MISSION

Young is a passionate supporter of causes close to his heart, including environmentalist issues, small farms – for which he co-founded Farm Aid in 1985 – and children with disabilities, for whom he helped to set up a specialist school the year after, in 1986.

MUSICAL STYLE
Country rock,
folk, noise rock

KEY DATES
Born in 1945

PEACE ACTIVIST

Anti-nuclear Young went
on to co-direct and star in
Human Highway, which was
set against the backdrop of
a nuclear power plant.

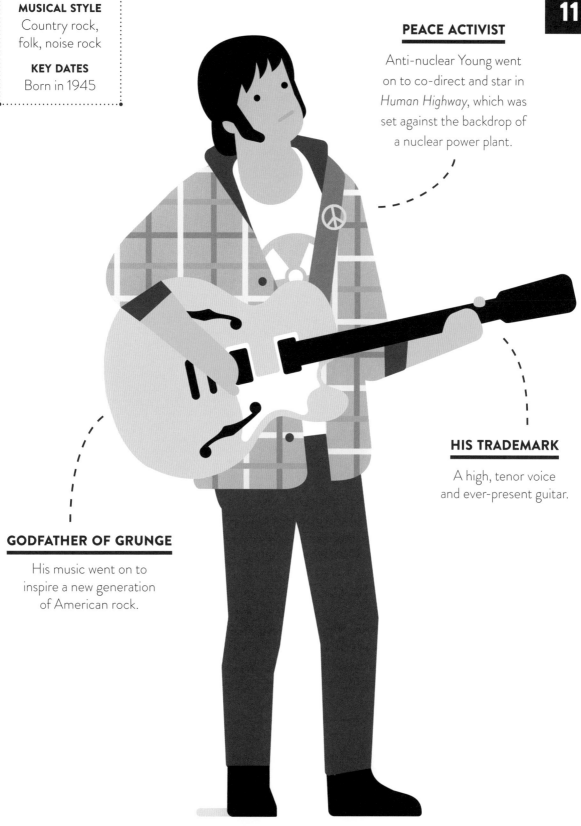

HIS TRADEMARK

A high, tenor voice
and ever-present guitar.

GODFATHER OF GRUNGE

His music went on to
inspire a new generation
of American rock.

The Loner

Led Zeppelin

Led Zeppelin set out on a sonic highway between hard rock and heavy metal after guitarist Jimmy Page tired of the repetitive blues at the heart of the band's earlier incarnation as the Yardbirds. He established a new line-up, with Robert Plant providing vocals, John Bonham on drums and John Paul Jones on bass, and began to bring new influences to their music, including folk, Eastern-sounding melodies and prog rock, which helped them to become one of the most iconic heavy metal groups to emerge from 1970s Britain.

John Paul Jones is a multi-instrumentist, playing bass and keys in the group. He can also play the violin, organ, sitar, cello, continuum, and recorder, among other instruments!

CONCERT

The band reunited for a concert in London in 2007, after nearly 30 years apart. The Celebration Day concert brought an audience of 20,000 fans back together again.

SELECTED DISCOGRAPHY

1969
Led Zeppelin

1971
Led Zeppelin IV

1975
Physical Graffiti

1994
No Quarter: Unledded

2012
Celebration Day (live)

QUITE A MAN

A brilliant drummer onstage, but self-destructive off, John Bonham's early death led to the break-up of Led Zeppelin. They didn't get back together again until twenty-seven years later, when Bonham's son, Jason, picked up his sticks and took his father's place.

EASTERN MOMENT

In 1994, Jimmy Page and Robert Plant came back to the fore with the magnificent *No Quarter*, an acoustic session with Arabic musicians, where they performed many of Led Zeppelin's best-loved hits, including a classic version of 'Kashmir'.

MUSICAL STYLE
Heavy metal,
hard rock

KEY DATES
Group began in
1968, split up
in 1980

ALCHEMY
Robert Plant's high-pitched
voice helped establish him as
the 'greatest metal vocalist of
all time'.

AN UNUSUAL UNIVERSE
The three intersecting circles
on John Bonham's bass drum
appeared on their album *Led
Zeppelin IV*.

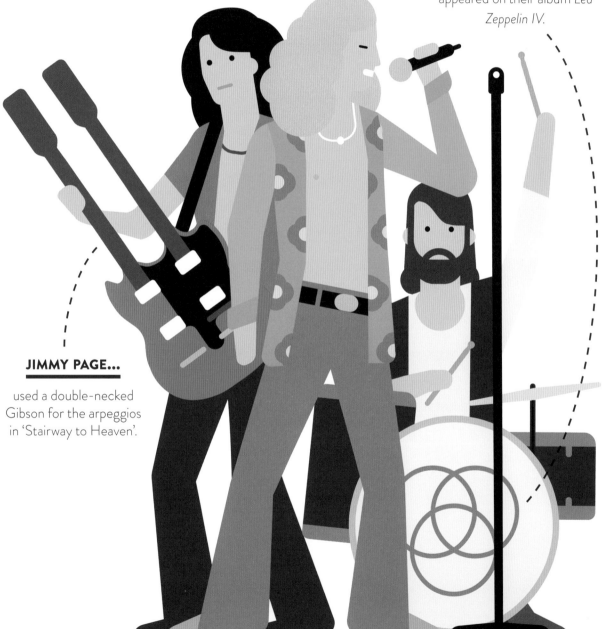

JIMMY PAGE...
used a double-necked
Gibson for the arpeggios
in 'Stairway to Heaven'.

Hammer of the Gods

David Bowie

The master of reinvention, David Bowie created some of the most innovative music and iconic characters that pop music has ever seen. Emerging on the scene during the glam rock era, he made the most of his androgynous appearance, adopting shocking red hair and painting a thunderbolt stripe on his face to steal the limelight as alter-ego 'Ziggy Stardust'. Over the next four decades, he would recast himself as the 'Thin White Duke' and 'Major Tom', pioneer new styles of music, and redefine pop history forever.

EXPERIMENTATION

Well before he worked with Daft Punk, Nile Rodgers, a disco funk guitarist, worked with Bowie on Bowie's best selling album: *Let's Dance*.

5 DATES

1969
First hit, 'Space Oddity'

1977-79
Records three albums in Berlin

1983
Big international success:
Let's Dance

1992
Married Somali model Iman

2016
Died, having released *Blackstar* just two days before

MAJOR ALBUM

Between 1977 and 1979, Bowie recorded three albums, which became known as 'the Berlin trilogy' and gave his fans a taste of electronic music: *Low, Heroes* and *Lodger*.

SIGN OF THE TIMES

Bowie's career is a kaleidoscope of musical trends: from his pop beginnings, he moved through glam rock (*Ziggy Stardust*), funk, new wave (with Brian Eno), dance (*Let's Dance*), garage rock (*Tin Machine*), and techno (*Outside*)... always with spectacular results.

RENAISSANCE MAN

Although he dedicated his life to music – releasing new albums right up until his death – Bowie was also a talented actor, starring in several avant-garde films, as well as an accomplished painter.

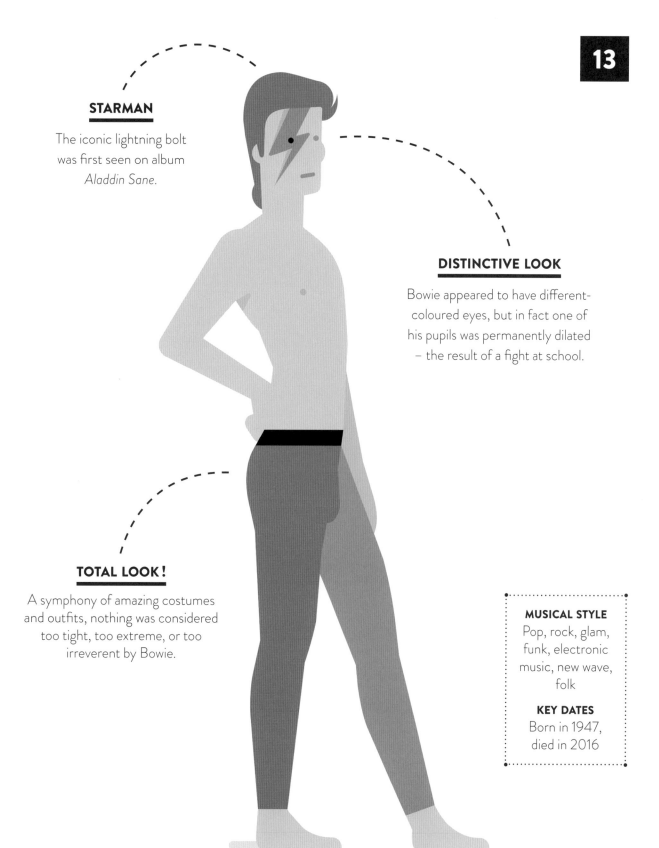

STARMAN

The iconic lightning bolt was first seen on album *Aladdin Sane.*

DISTINCTIVE LOOK

Bowie appeared to have different-coloured eyes, but in fact one of his pupils was permanently dilated – the result of a fight at school.

TOTAL LOOK !

A symphony of amazing costumes and outfits, nothing was considered too tight, too extreme, or too irreverent by Bowie.

MUSICAL STYLE
Pop, rock, glam, funk, electronic music, new wave, folk

KEY DATES
Born in 1947, died in 2016

Ziggy

Queen

Moving between hard rock and pop operetta, British group Queen dominated the charts in the 1970s and 1980s with their varied hits and incredible live performances. Adored by fans, but panned by critics, Queen became internationally famous thanks not only to their powerful stadium anthems – heard on radios, in sports venues, and in West-End theatres the world over – but also their legendary frontman, Freddie Mercury, who remains one of the most outstanding performers in rock history.

STADIUM ROCK

Taking to the stage with big hair, big voices, and really big guitars, Queen defined the stadium rock genre. They created hits such as 'We Will Rock You' and 'We Are the Champions' with the idea that a huge audience could join in... and boy, did they respond!

CONCERT

Queen will be forever remembered for stealing the show with the incredible set they performed at Live Aid, a charity event watched by more than two billion people in 60 different countries.

5 DATES

1973
First album with EMI

1975
'Bohemian Rhapsody'

1977
'We Will Rock You', 'We Are the Champions'

1981
'Under Pressure' with David Bowie

1991
Death of Freddie Mercury

BITTERSWEET

After Mercury's early death (due to complications from AIDS) Brian May commented, "Now, the critics say that Freddie Mercury was amazing, that there was no performer like him but let's remember – they didn't say any of that when we were just starting out."

MUSICAL STYLE
Glam rock,
prog rock

KEY DATES
Mostly active
from 1971 to 1991

COSTUMES

The band flaunted their
eccentric, ostentatious
costumes... especially
Freddie!

HIS VOICE

Mercury wrote many
of the band's best hits,
including the epic,
six-minute 'Bohemian
Rhapsody'.

QUEEN

Originally called Smile,
Mercury later suggested
the name 'Queen',
saying, "It's a strong
name, very universal and
immediate."

Glam rock

Michael Jackson

The King of Pop had humble beginnings, growing up alongside seven siblings in a two-bed house in Indiana. But a combination of hard work and once-in-a-generation talent produced one of the most incredible musical careers of the 20th century, making Michael Jackson the archetype of the American dream. Outshining his brothers in the Jackson 5, aged just six, he was an outstanding dancer, a mind-blowing choreographer, inspired songwriter and a performer without equal. His early death in 2009 sent shock waves throughout the world.

EXPERIMENTATION

Jackson pioneered the use of video in the pop genre, transforming it into an art form, experimenting with storylines, dance routines and special effects.

SIGNATURE MOVES

Through his onstage and video performances, Michael Jackson immortalised, a number of eye-popping dance techniques, such as the 'robot', the 'crotch grab', the 'anti-gravity lean' and, perhaps most famously, the 'moonwalk'.

TROUBLED GENIUS

Jackson's life wasn't without controversy – perhaps the result of an unhappy childhood. His dramatically changing appearance, troubled private life and legal disputes were made much of by the media, causing him to become reclusive in later years.

MAJOR ALBUM

Thriller, produced by long-time Jackson collaborator Quincy Jones, has sold a whopping 66 million copies, making it the best-selling album of all time.

SLICK LOOK

Jackson's hairstyle changed with the times. Sporting an afro in his youth, he wore his hair in silky locks later in his career.

MUSICAL STYLE
Mix of pop, funk and soul

KEY DATES
Born in 1958, died in 2009

DRESSED TO KILL

Jackson's influence on fashion is undeniable. Borrowing looks from the military, bikers and speakeasy gangsters to name a few, he set many new trends.

FANCY FOOTWORK

Jackson wore short trousers, black mocassins and white socks to enhance the visual effect of his dance moves.

The King of Pop

ABBA

Bursting onto the scene at the 1974 Eurovision song contest, the Stockholm-based pop group's winning song 'Waterloo' was soon topping the charts worldwide. And this was just the beginning – throughout the decade, ABBA set the bar with their commercial brand of Europop, pumping out catchy melodies, clever arrangements, and memorable lyrics. Parodied for much of the 1980s, the group later enjoyed a revival and were honoured at the 50th anniversary celebration of the Eurovision Song Contest, where their journey began.

Over
400
million records sold!

BACKGROUND

ABBA came from Sweden, but sang mostly in English – and sometimes in Spanish, French and German, too – which gave them international appeal.

5 DATES

1966
Björn and Benny's first song

1970
ABBA is created

1974 'Waterloo' wins the Eurovision Song Contest

1976
'Dancing Queen'. World domination

1982
ABBA split up

TWO COUPLES

The group was made up of two couples: Agnetha and Björn, and Benny and Anni-Frid. Together, the initials of their names made up the group's name, ABBA. Sadly, both couples ended up divorcing, leading to the band's break-up in 1982.

THRIFTY LOOK

Summing up seventies style with their flamboyant loons, cheeky hotpants, high-necked shirts and use of glitter, the band adopted their outrageous look because Swedish tax laws dictated that their clothes mustn't be appropriate to wear offstage!

PALINDROMIC

Agnetha Fältskog was already a successful solo act in Sweden before she joined the group.

COUPLES

Together, Björn Ulvaeus and Benny Andersson made a pop-writing powerhouse.

COSTUMES

ABBA's music was famously used in *Muriel's Wedding*, *Priscilla Queen of the Desert* and *Mamma Mia!*

ABBA

MUSICAL STYLE
Pop, pop and more pop

KEY DATES
Active between 1972 and 1982

Ultimate Europop

Bob Marley

MAJOR ALBUM

Exodus was in the British charts for 56 weeks back to back, and established his reputation worldwide.

Robert Nesta 'Bob' Marley inspired a love of reggae – and Jamaican culture – in millions around the world. Infusing his music with Trenchtown's native ska, rocksteady, and reggae, he created his own unique 'Rastaman's Vibration', which helped to make him an icon around the world. He became a committed Rastafarian – a political and spiritual movement which began in Jamaica in 1930s – and used his status to promote a message of freedom, peace and unity against a backdrop of political turmoil.

FAMILY AFFAIR

Dying at the young age of just 36, while he was still at the height of his powers, Marley was survived by his eleven children – two of whom (Damian and Ziggy) are talented musicians in their own rights, and who ensured his legacy would live on.

5 DATES

1962
First single, 'One Cup of Coffee'

1973
First album, *Catch a Fire*

1975
'No Woman, No Cry' gives Marley his first taste of international fame

1980
Last album, *Uprising*

1981
Died in Miami

THE WAILERS

Marley originally started out as 'Bob Marley & the Wailers', and accompanied by his wife, Rita, he combined important themes with melodious reggae and hard-hitting lyrics – 'Redemption Song' being the perfect example.

BACKGROUND

The identity of Bob Marley and Jamaica will forever be interlinked; you can't talk about one without thinking about the other.

NATTY DREAD

Marley's dreadlocks are a trademark of his religion, Rastafarianism.

MUSICAL STYLE
Ska, rocksteady then reggae

KEY DATES
Born in 1945, died in 1981

GREEN, YELLOW

AND RED

The colours synonymous with Marley, and reggae, who were both born in Jamaica.

ONE LOVE

Marley sent out a strong message of love and tolerance.

One Love

AC/DC

AC/DC's brand of hard rock may have its roots down under, but it quickly found a devoted audience around the world. Founded by two brothers, Malcolm and Angus Young, the band's line-up changed many times over the years, most notably when Bon Scott, their lead singer, died, leaving the band devastated. But, having recruited a new frontman, Brian Johnson, the band released their seminal album *Back in Black*, and the group – still together – still has a devoted fanbase across the world to this day.

BACKGROUND

The band are Australian – or more precisely Sydneysiders – but originally hail from Glasgow in Scotland.

MAJOR ALBUM

Back in Black has sold 50 million copies – the second highest sales of any album in the world after Michael Jackson's *Thriller*.

TOTALLY ELECTRIC

Having seen the letters 'AC/DC' on a household appliance, the Youngs' older sister Margaret suggested using it for the name of their group. It stands for 'alternating current/direct current', and inspired the name of their first album, *High Voltage*.

MUSICAL WEAPON

In 1989, having failed to draw General Manuel Noriega out of his compound in Panama by force, the U.S. military tried a new technique… They blared AC/DC music outside his camp for two continuous days. The dictator surrendered.

SELECTED DISCOGRAPHY

1977
Let There Be Rock

1978
If You Want Blood, You've Got It (live)

1979
Highway to Hell

1980
Back in Black

2008
Black Ice

MUSICAL STYLE
Hard rock,
blues rock

KEY DATES
Group formed
in 1973

THE SCHOOL BOY

Angus went straight from
school to rehearse... and
his uniform became his
costume!

BON'S STORY

The first singer of the group, the
charismatic Bon Scott
was also originally from Scotland...
as were his bagpipes!

TWO BROTHERS

Brothers Malcolm
and Angus Young
were the founding
members of
the group.

Let There Be Rock

Patti Smith

'**Punk poet laureate**' Patricia Lee 'Patti' Smith established herself as a major name in the 1970s. Thanks to her talent for blending poetry with art rock, she became a staple of the New York art scene, where she hung out with the elite artists of the time: poet Allen Ginsberg, photographer Robert Mapplethorpe (whom she dated), playwright and actor Sam Shepard, and John Cale (of Velvet Underground fame) were all close friends. Proving that rock wasn't just for guys, she was later dubbed 'godmother of punk rock'.

A modern-day Rennaissance woman, more recently Smith has put on a series of exhibitions of her photographs.

INFLUENCE

Inspired by poets like Rimbaud, Blake, Nerval and Baudelaire, Patti Smith has had her own poems published.

JUST KIDS

Honouring a promise she made to Mapplethorpe on his deathbed, Patti Smith went on to write her memoirs, titling the book *Just Kids*. It went on to establish her literary reputation and won the National Book Award for Nonfiction.

PEOPLE HAVE THE POWER

Smith remains true to her anthem 'People Have the Power'. An active supporter of a multitude of causes, she uses her platform to promote her liberal stance on political and environmental issues.

5 DATES

1978
'Because the Night'

1979
'Frederick'

1988
'People Have the Power'

2010
Just Kids
(autobiography, 1st part)

2015
M Train
(autobiography, 2nd part)

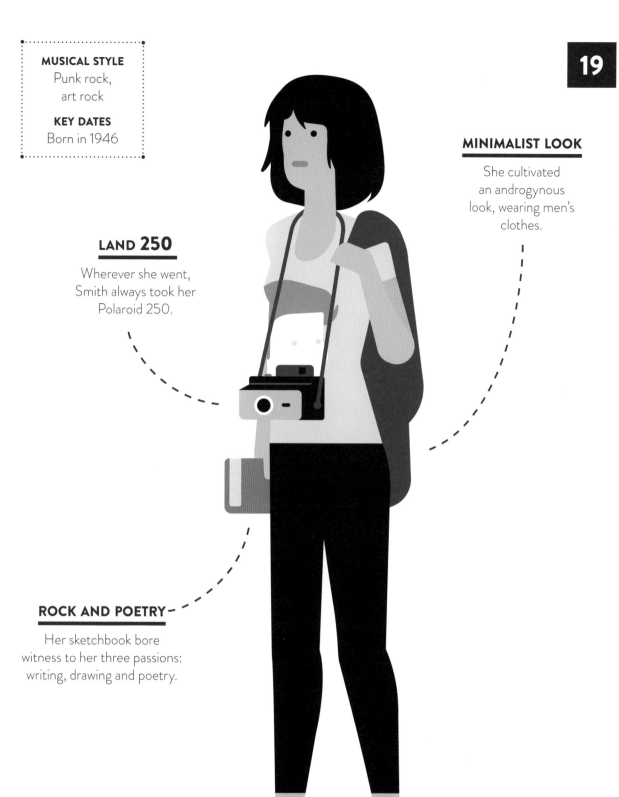

19

MUSICAL STYLE
Punk rock,
art rock

KEY DATES
Born in 1946

MINIMALIST LOOK

She cultivated
an androgynous
look, wearing men's
clothes.

LAND 250

Wherever she went,
Smith always took her
Polaroid 250.

ROCK AND POETRY

Her sketchbook bore
witness to her three passions:
writing, drawing and poetry.

Punk Poet Laureate

Blondie

Chris Stein and Debbie Harry discovered each other on America's underground scene in the middle of the 1970s. It was instant attraction... and the beginning of Blondie! Soon regular performers at New York's CBGB club, three revolutionary albums followed, one after the other. Fusing disco rock, new wave, punk, reggae and rap, Blondie, soon began to enjoy major commercial success and the photogenic Debbie Harry – one of the first women to lead a rock group – became a punk icon.

over **40** million albums sold!

BACKGROUND

The group comes from New York, home to CBGB, the legendary club at the forefront of the alternative American music scene of the 1970s.

SELECTED DISCOGRAPHY

1978
Plastic Letters

1978
Parallel Lines

1979
Eat to the Beat

1999
No Exit

2014
Blondie 4(0) Ever

LIVING ART

Andy Warhol immortalised Debbie Harry when he painted her portrait in 1980 after they crossed paths on Broadway and 13th Street in New York. It was sold at auction for several million euros.

PAUSE

In 1983, Chris Stein fell seriously ill. He was diagnosed with a rare autoimmune skin condition, causing Blondie to disband. But, in 1997, they reformed, and were soon back at the top of the charts – exactly twenty years after the band's first number one.

20

MUSICAL STYLE
Pop, post-punk, reggae, disco

KEY DATES
Active from 1975 to 1982

CHRIS STEIN
Guitar player and co-founder of the group and, for a while, Debbie Harry's boyfriend.

DEBBIE HARRY
Her looks caused people to call out in the street, "Hey, blondie!"... hence the group's name.

PARALLEL LINES
This album was their biggest success.

Blondies have more fun

Sex Pistols

EXPERIMENTATION

They sparked the punk movement, with a new way of being, of expressing themselves and of rebelling in music.

Forming in London in 1975, the Sex Pistols ushered in a new era of punk in the UK with fire and brimstone. Standing for everything anti-establishment, the band's angry image and anarchistic message struck a chord with the disillusioned youth of '70s Britain, and their politicised tracks 'God Save the Queen' and 'Anarchy in the UK' sowed discord in their wake. Over three turbulent years, the band hit the headlines with their obscene lyrics, chaotic gigs and line-up changes, a period dubbed as the 'last and greatest outbreak of pop-based moral pandemonium'.

NEVER MIND

John 'Johnny Rotten' Lydon was asked to join the band after he was spotted wearing a T-shirt he had doctored to say 'I Hate Pink Floyd'. After the Sex Pistols disbanded, he founded post-punk band PiL (Public Image Limited).

5 DATES

1975
Sex Pistols formed

1978
Split up
in confusion

1979
Death of the bass
player Sid Vicious

1996 and 2006
Band reunites for
lucrative tours

2014
Autobiography
published of John
Lydon, former
leader of the group

CONCERT

In 1977, they performed on a boat going down the Thames during the Queen's Jubilee, and played 'Anarchy in the UK' opposite Parliament.

PUNK BOMB!

On 4 June 1976, the Sex Pistols set off a punk rock bomb when they performed in Manchester's Lesser Free Trade Hall. The venue was crammed with people who would go on to form their own influential rock groups: the Buzzcocks, Joy Division and the Fall.

21

MUSICAL STYLE
Punk

KEY DATES
The group formed
in 1975, and fell
apart in 1978

AGENTS OF ANARCHY

Adopting Vivienne Westwood's
look, their safety pins, torn T-shirts,
dog collars, chains, and messy hair
came to define the punk look.

FOUNDERS

Paul Cook (drummer)
and his childhood friend
Steve Jones.

"SEX PISTOLS"

The group's
guitarist, Steve
Jones, came up
with the name.

Pioneers of punk

The Clash

With their album *Sandinista!* they lent their support to the Sandinista movement in Nicaragua – and anticipated the trend for world music in the 1980s.

If the Sex Pistols were the masters of punk, the Clash – also from London – were the godfathers of post-punk. But, unlike the Sex Pistols, the band showed extreme discipline: they respected their fans, stuck to their contracts and remained true to themselves. Constantly experimenting with different musical genres, the group's primary songwriters, Joe Strummer and Mick Jones, combined controversial lyrics with unforgettable tunes, earning them the moniker 'the Only Band That Matters'.

LONDON CALLING!

A masterpiece of rebellion, 'London Calling' is a rally cry against unemployment and the politics of Margaret Thatcher. The Clash sold this double album for the price of a normal album, and waived their royalties – that pretty much sums the band up.

SELECTED DISCOGRAPHY

1977
The Clash

1978
Give 'Em Enough Rope

1979
London Calling

1980
Sandinista!

1982
Combat Rock

MORE THAN PUNK

Most of the band's debut LP, *The Clash*, was written in Mick's grandmother's 18th-floor council flat on London's Harrow Road. His grandmother was a great supporter of the band, and regularly came to their gigs!

"They were the biggest rock group. They led the way."

Bono, U2

DRESSED FOR COMBAT

Paint-spattered trousers, stencilled T-shirts and combat fatigues... the boys were ready for battle.

ROYAL RIP OFF

The cover of *London Calling* is a rip-off of Elvis's *Rock and Roll* LP of 1956.

ICONS

Joe Strummer, Mick Jones, Paul Simonon and Topper Headon, formed the classic line-up.

BRIGADE

RAF

ROSSE

MUSICAL STYLE
Pop rock, punk, rock, reggae, dub

KEY DATES
Group formed in 1976, split up in 1985

'The Only Band That Matters'

U2

Although they formed in 1976, Dubliners Bono, the Edge, Adam Clayton and Larry Mullen waited four years before they hit the big time with their first album, *Boy*. But their success snowballed over the next twenty years, and they became a global phenomenon, notching up hit after hit, and winning endless awards. Electrifying huge arenas with their live performances, the band subsequently lent their Midas touch to several blockbuster movies, writing music for *Goldeneye* and *Mission: Impossible*.

MAJOR ALBUM

The Joshua Tree, released in 1987, shot U2 to international stardom, and gave the band their only number-one singles in the U.S.: 'With or Without You' and 'I Still Haven't Found What I'm Looking For'.

5 DATES

1983
War

1984
The Unforgettable Fire

1987
The Joshua Tree

1991
Achtung Baby

1995
Members of U2 associated with Brian Eno as the Passengers

SUNDAY BLOODY SUNDAY

War, released in 1983, assured U2's notoriety. It opened with the track, 'Sunday Bloody Sunday', which relates to the events of 30 January 1972, in Londonderry, when 14 Catholics taking part in a civil rights demonstration were shot by the British Army.

U2?

Does U2 refer to a Soviet biplane, a U.S. reconnaissance aircraft, a German submarine, a type of battery, a clothing line...? Or does it mean 'You too' or even 'You two'? Ask the advertiser who came up with the name! Either way, Bono hated the name!

ACTIVISM

In 1985, the group took part in Live Aid, a benefit concert to raise money for those suffering from famine in Africa. They also spoke out against the arms race, apartheid, El Salvador, and AIDS.

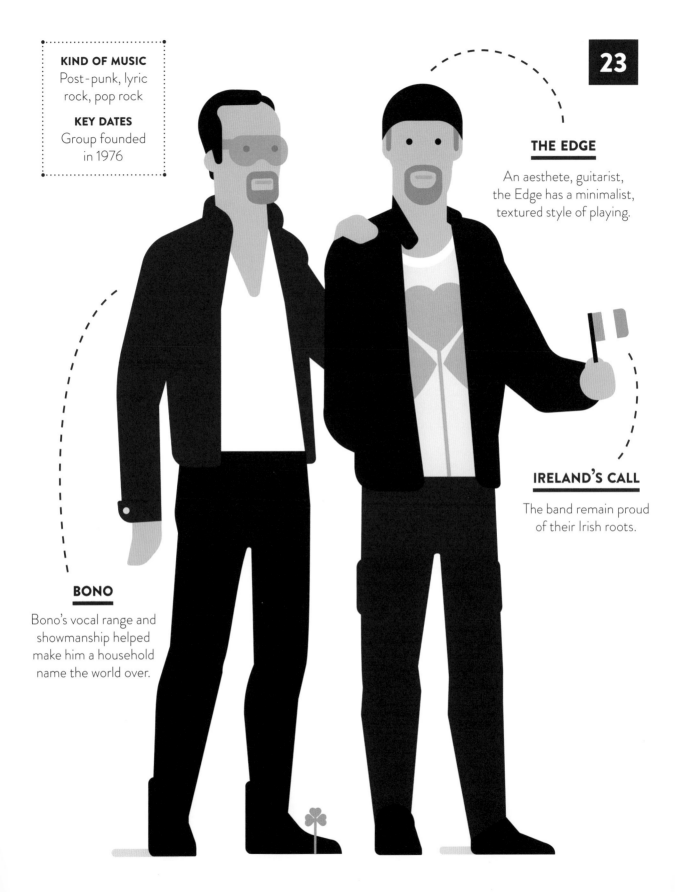

THE EDGE
An aesthete, guitarist, the Edge has a minimalist, textured style of playing.

IRELAND'S CALL
The band remain proud of their Irish roots.

BONO
Bono's vocal range and showmanship helped make him a household name the world over.

Bono Vox

The Police

Credited with leading the Second British Invasion of the US, today, London-based group the Police are recognised as one of the best groups of the post-punk scene, every bit as influential as U2 and the Cure. With hits like 'Roxanne', 'Message in a Bottle', 'So Lonely' and 'Every Breath You Take', you just have to look at the Police's long back catalogue to get a sense of their huge popularity. With a talent for combining melody with technique, they notched up five consecutive No. 1 albums in the UK.

CORSICA

Sting called time on the band at the end of their Synchronicity tour in 1984. Tempers flared as the bandmembers shared new songwriting ideas; as Sting said, "It's difficult to tell somebody it's not a good song, and it was usually me."

CONCERT

Having disbanded in 1986, fans flocked when they reformed for a triumphant reunion tour, which took place in 2006 and 2007.

SELECTED DISCOGRAPHY

1978
Outlandos d'Amour

1979
Regatta de Blanc

1980
Zenyatta Mondatta

1981
Ghost in the Machine

1983
Synchronicity

TRUE PROS

The band's strength lay with the trio's technical ability. Copeland was a seasoned drummer; Sting was an accomplished jazz bass player; and Summers was a professional guitar player, having already played with numerous groups.

ACTIVISM

Before joining the Police, Sting was already politically engaged and today he continues to fight for causes including the Amazon rainforest and human rights.

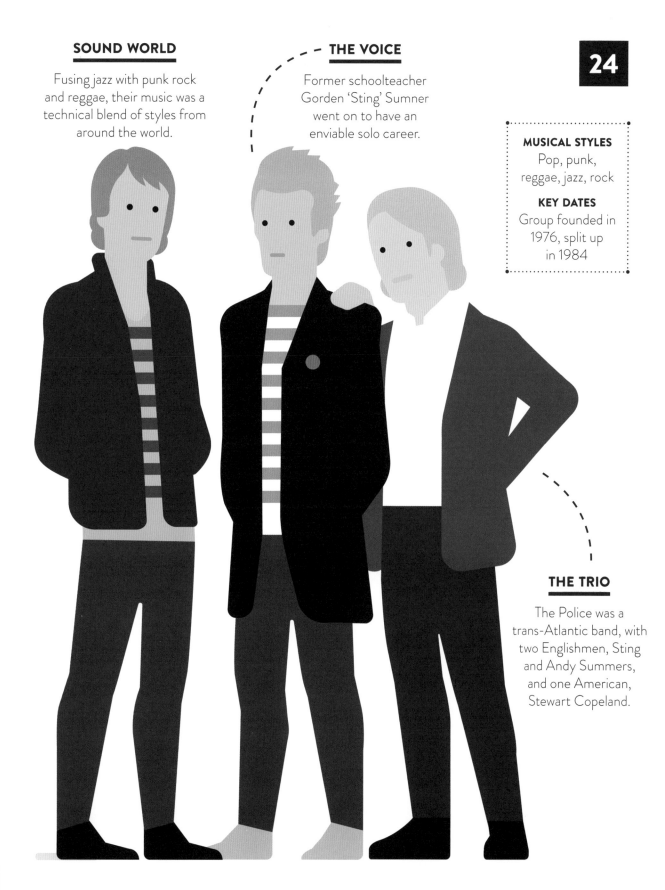

SOUND WORLD

Fusing jazz with punk rock and reggae, their music was a technical blend of styles from around the world.

THE VOICE

Former schoolteacher Gorden 'Sting' Sumner went on to have an enviable solo career.

MUSICAL STYLES
Pop, punk, reggae, jazz, rock

KEY DATES
Group founded in 1976, split up in 1984

THE TRIO

The Police was a trans-Atlantic band, with two Englishmen, Sting and Andy Summers, and one American, Stewart Copeland.

Power pop trio

The Cure

CONCERT

The group's performances at the Orange amphitheatre in 1986 were made into a film – *The Cure in Orange*. It marked the beginning of a series of stadium concerts.

Robert Smith was undeniably the heart of English band the Cure, being its main songwriter and its only consistent member through several line-up changes. Steering the band through varying phases, including gothic rock, post-punk, alternative rock and new wave, his astonishingly inventive writing won him a dedicated following of fans. Initially embracing dark, tormented themes, his writing became increasingly lighter and more romantic over the years, while he himself became the icon of a generation.

TRILOGY

Seventeen Seconds, *Faith* and *Pornography*, released in consecutive years between 1980 and 1982, symbolise the group's creative and emotional pinnacle. Radical, dark, cold and depressive, they were also fascinating and moving.

SELECTED DISCOGRAPHY

1980
Seventeen Seconds

1981
Faith

1982
Pornography

1985
The Head on the Door

1989
Disintegration

INFLUENCE

The Cure was influenced by Jimi Hendrix, the Doors and David Bowie, but also by groups like Captain Beefheart, Joy Division and the Wire.

HITTING THE BIGTIME

Back-to back sell-out shows at Wembley Stadium and New York's Giants Stadium gave the Cure a claim to being the biggest band in the world in 1989. "It was never our intention to become as big as this," rued Smith.

25

MUSICAL STYLES
New wave, gothic, then pop

KEY DATES
Group began in 1976 (with the name 'Easy Cure')

ROBERT SMITH
With his smeared lipstick and backcombed hair, Smith became a symbol of the new wave.

SIMON GALLUP
Gallup's playing brought the bass guitar to the fore, making it more than just an accompanying instrument.

CUREMANIA
In the 1980s, fans copied the Cure's black goth look.

The goth hit machine

Depeche Mode

English electronic band Depeche Mode were modern pop incarnate. Storming their way onto the British new wave scene with their innovative use of technology and sampling, they put out 53 singles over the course of their career. They also released eight remix compilations, pioneering a new genre of alternative versions, remixing techno, dance and rock. With Martin Gore's cutting-edge songwriting and Dave Gahan's powerful voice, Depeche Mode became a huge act around the world in the 1990s.

INSTRUMENTS

Martin Gore did his songwriting on the guitar before translating them onto the synthesiser.

FASHIONABLE NAME

Originally called Composition of Sound, the band changed to Dépêche mode in 1980, borrowing the name from a French fashion magazine. Explaining the choice, Gore said, "It means hurried fashion or fashion dispatch. I like the sound of that."

ESSEX BOYS

Depeche Mode were from Basildon in Essex, as were Vince Clarke and Alison Moyet, founder and singer respectively of Yazoo – another synth-pop group that was also very successful in the 1980s.

Over

75

million albums sold in the world!

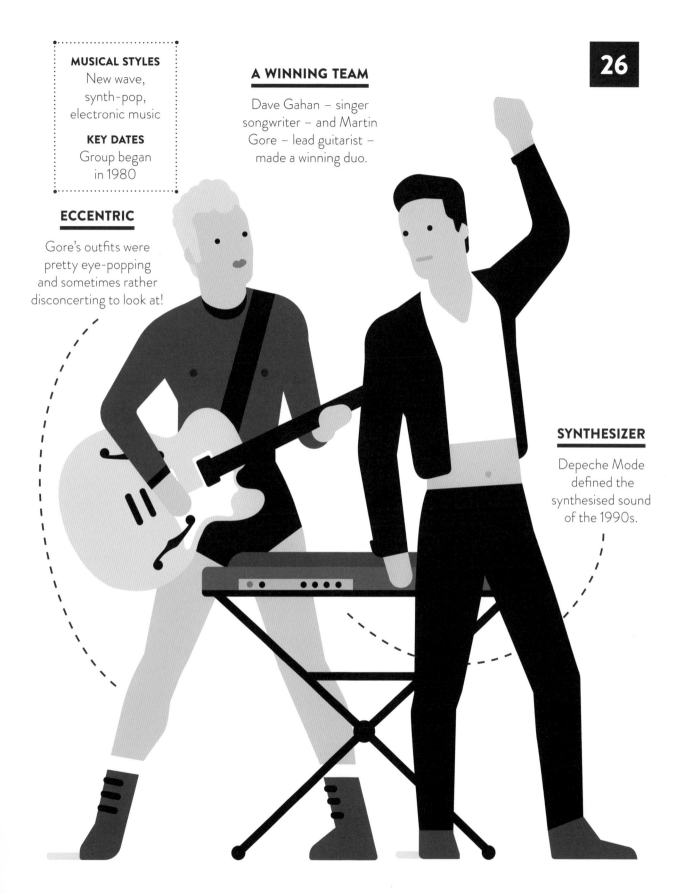

26

MUSICAL STYLES
New wave,
synth-pop,
electronic music

KEY DATES
Group began
in 1980

A WINNING TEAM

Dave Gahan – singer
songwriter – and Martin
Gore – lead guitarist –
made a winning duo.

ECCENTRIC

Gore's outfits were
pretty eye-popping
and sometimes rather
disconcerting to look at!

SYNTHESIZER

Depeche Mode
defined the
synthesised sound
of the 1990s.

Music for the Masses

New Order

INSTRUMENTS

The omnipresent drum 'n' bass by Peter Hook and Stephen Morris was a model of the genre.

English band New Order made their name in the 1980s with their unique mix of emotional yet 'cold' dance music, combining post-punk with electronic and dance music. The group arose from the ashes of legendary post-punk group Joy Division following the death of their lead singer, Ian Curtis. They went on to define a new era of pop, putting out several tracks that remain classics to this day, most notably 'Blue Monday', which still stands as the best-selling extended single of all time.

SHOT OF INSPIRATION

Sumner and Hook were among the crowd at the Sex Pistols' legendary show at the Manchester Lesser Free Trade Hall. The morning after the gig, Hook borrowed £35 from his mother to buy his first bass guitar.

SELECTED DISCOGRAPHY

1983
Power, Corruption and Lies

1985
Low-Life

1987
Substance (compilation)

1989
Technique

2012
Live at Bestival

BACKGROUND

The members of New Order were from Manchester, the city which spawned 'Madchester' in the 1980s, with superclub the Haçienda at its heart.

DESIGN

New Order used the minimalist designer Peter Saville almost exclusively to design their album covers, which didn't feature the name of the album or even the group. The design for 'Blue Monday' was so expensive to produce that the band lost money with every sale!

27

MUSICAL STYLES
New wave, dance, pop

KEY DATES
Group began in 1980

WITH CALCULATED ANONYMITY...

... and mysterious album covers, they were ahead of their time.

TRUE PIONEER

A true pioneer of new technology, Sumner created his own sequencers to link the synth and drum tracks.

PLAY IT AGAIN!

Never fans of the encore, the group sparked a riot when they refused to play one at the height of their 'Blue Monday' fame.

JOY DIVISION

The 'non-image' band

The Smiths

Calling themselves the Smiths (the most common name in Britain) in contrast to more pompous band names around at the time, this English pop group, like New Order, formed in Manchester in the 1980s. But the group renounced the synthesised pop sound dominating the charts at the time, and instead adopted a simple line-up of guitar, bass, and drum, fusing rock and post-punk influences to create a romantic yet cynical music that owes everything to its two founding members: Morrissey and Johnny Marr.

MAJOR ALBUM

For many people, *The Queen Is Dead*, which came out in 1986, is the pinnacle of English pop.

BACKGROUND

The members of the group are from Manchester and inspired later bands from the same city, including the Stone Roses and Oasis.

GOING SOLO

After the break-up of the group, Morrissey launched himself as a solo artist and garnered an even greater following. Meanwhile, Johnny Marr went on to collaborate with other artists, including the Pretenders, and New Order's Bernard Sumner.

MEAT IS MURDER

Morrissey has been vegetarian since he was 11 and championed the cause through his album title *Meat Is Murder*. He even forbade the other members of the group from being photographed while eating meat.

SELECTED DISCOGRAPHY

1984
The Smiths

1985
Meat Is Murder

1986
The Queen Is Dead

1987
Strangeways, Here We Come

1988
Rank (live)

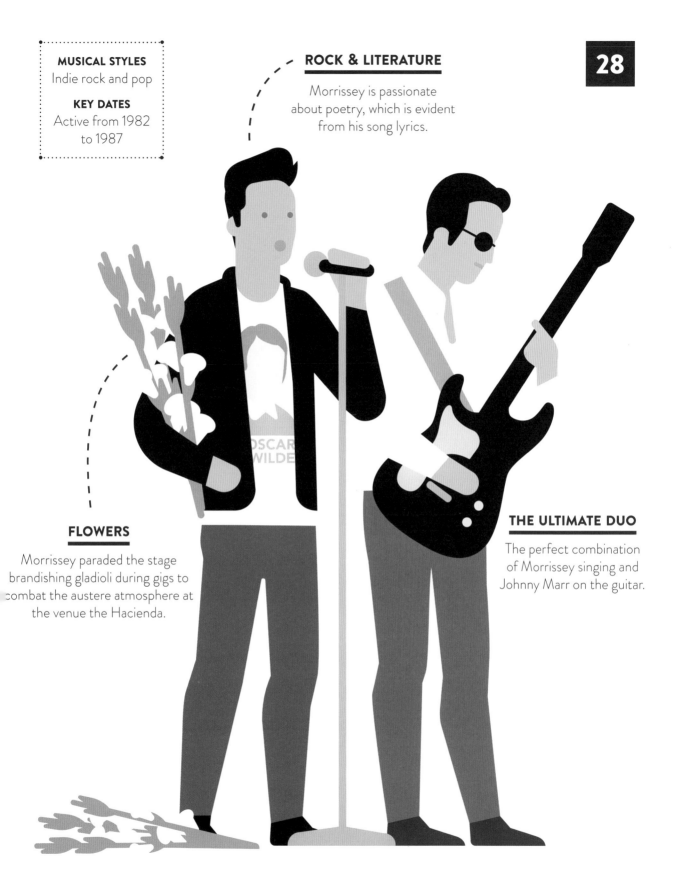

28

MUSICAL STYLES
Indie rock and pop

KEY DATES
Active from 1982 to 1987

ROCK & LITERATURE

Morrissey is passionate about poetry, which is evident from his song lyrics.

FLOWERS

Morrissey paraded the stage brandishing gladioli during gigs to combat the austere atmosphere at the venue the Hacienda.

THE ULTIMATE DUO

The perfect combination of Morrissey singing and Johnny Marr on the guitar.

The indie outsiders

Madonna

'**Madonna**' **Louise Ciccone** set out on her quest for stardom when she moved to New York in 1977. She was soon signed by a major label and released her eponymous debut album in 1985. With a musical palette that included dance, pop, electronic music, rock and swing, she became known as a chameleon with a talent for reinventing her music, and her look, over and again. Still a prominent figure within popular culture today, the so-called Queen of Pop's influence can be felt beyond music, in the realms of film, fashion and art.

MAJOR ALBUM

True Blue, her third album, sold 25 million copies and is still her best-selling studio album.

5 DATES

1977
First dance classes in New York

1983
First album, *Madonna*

1985
First leading role in a film: *Desperately Seeking Susan*

1997
85 different outfits for the film *Evita!*

2012
38th entry in the top 10 of *Billboard's Hot 100*, a record for any artist.

CONCERT

Madonna is also the highest-earning solo touring artist of all time. She has made U.S. $1.4 billion from her concert ticket sales alone.

POWER POP

Competing against wave after wave of new pop acts, Madonna has managed to retain her relevance and popularity with new generations of pop fans, and today she is recognized as the best-selling female recording artist of all time.

FILM STAR

As well as becoming a global music icon, Madonna has made a name for herself in the cinema as an actor and director, winning a Golden Globe Award for Best Actress for her portrayal of Eva Perón in the 1996 film *Evita*.

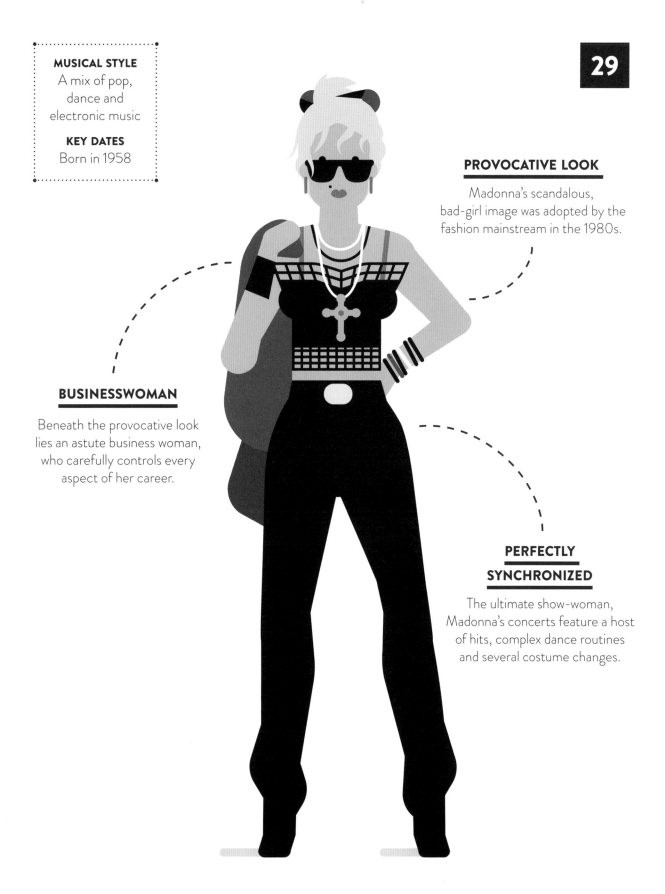

29

MUSICAL STYLE
A mix of pop, dance and electronic music

KEY DATES
Born in 1958

PROVOCATIVE LOOK
Madonna's scandalous, bad-girl image was adopted by the fashion mainstream in the 1980s.

BUSINESSWOMAN
Beneath the provocative look lies an astute business woman, who carefully controls every aspect of her career.

PERFECTLY SYNCHRONIZED
The ultimate show-woman, Madonna's concerts feature a host of hits, complex dance routines and several costume changes.

The Queen of Pop

Red Hot Chili Peppers

Forging their own style of rock, Los Angeles-based group Red Hot Chili Peppers have been igniting stadium audiences for decades with their uplifting brand of funk metal. Popular since the beginning of the 1990s, the band changed direction in the noughties, taking a more conventional path, writing commercial tunes and even pop ballads. Nevertheless they remained enormously successful, with more number-one singles and the most number of cumulative weeks at number one to their name in the U.S. than any band in history.

EXPERIMENTATION

is the trademark of Red Hot Chili Peppers, as they play with rock, funk, punk, metal and rap in their music.

SELECTED DISCOGRAPHY

1991
Blood Sugar Sex Magik

1999
Californication

2002
By the Way

2004
Live in Hyde Park (live)

2006
Stadium Arcadium

TRANSITION

Following the death of lead guitarist Hillel Slovak in 1988, a succession of musicians filled the role, notably Dave Navarro and John Frusciante, before Josh Klinghoffer took the post, later becoming the youngest artist ever to be inducted into the hall of fame.

CARTOON CHARACTERS

The band were immortalised in animated form when they made an appearance in an episode of the classic cartoon *The Simpsons* playing 'Give It Away' in their underwear during 'Krusty Gets Cancelled'.

BACKGROUND

The Chili Peppers are all fans of their local basketball team, the Los Angeles Lakers.

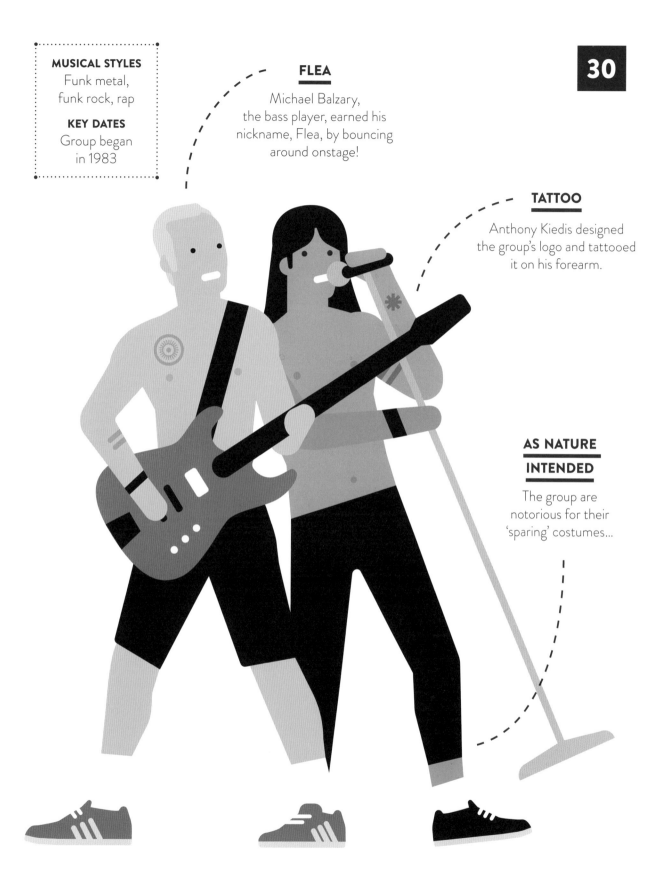

30

MUSICAL STYLES
Funk metal,
funk rock, rap

KEY DATES
Group began
in 1983

FLEA
Michael Balzary,
the bass player, earned his
nickname, Flea, by bouncing
around onstage!

TATTOO
Anthony Kiedis designed
the group's logo and tattooed
it on his forearm.

AS NATURE
INTENDED
The group are
notorious for their
'sparing' costumes...

Hot funk rock!

N.W.A

MAJOR ALBUM

Straight Outta Compton (1988)
was the original
gangsta rap album.

The tornado that was N.W.A took California — and the rest of the U.S. — by storm towards the end of the 1980s. This collective of talented and hard-hitting rappers included Eazy-E, Dr Dre and Ice Cube, and heralded the birth of gangsta rap, a controversial genre criticised for its explicit lyrics, sexism towards women, and glorification of crime. The fall-out between Dr Dre and Eazy-E caused the group to break up in 1991, but following Easy-E's death, they later reunited to make the biographical film *Straight Outta Compton*.

G-FUNK

With their second album, producer Dr Dre layed down the foundations for G-Funk — or gangsta funk — a subgenre of hip-hop music influenced by the local Californian sound, featuring fewer samples and a 'lazy', slower style of rapping.

5 DATES

1986
Eazy-E established the group

1988
Straight Outta Compton

1991
Released their final album, then disbanded

1995
Death of Eazy-E

2015
Film released *N.W.A: Straight Outta Compton*

BACKGROUND

N.W.A formed in Compton, a deprived neighbourhood in downtown Los Angeles. Their biographical film *Straight Outta Compton* documents the group's rise and fall.

DR DRE & ICE CUBE

After N.W.A, Dr Dre went on to become a sought-after hip-hop producer, and the mastermind behind Beats, a new brand of headphones. Aside fom his rapping career, Ice Cube went on to be a scriptwriter, actor and producer.

31

MUSICAL STYLES
Hip-hop, West
Coast rap, gangsta
rap

KEY DATES
Group was active
from 1986 to 1991

FAMOUS FIVE
The collective was formed of
rappers Ice Cube, Eazy-E and
MC Ren producer Dr Dre
and DJ Yella.

DRESS CODE
The group embodied
West Coast street style, wearing
'snapbacks' (a kind of cap)
and Oakland Raiders T-shirts.

EAZY-E
Eazy-E came to
be known as 'the
Godfather of
Gangsta rap.'

Ice-cool hip-hop

Pixies

Considered the forerunners of grunge, American alt rock band the Pixies was born when Black Francis met Joey Santiago, and were later joined by Kim Deal and David Lovering. Fans admired their original sound, which combined elements of psychedelia, noise pop, hard rock, and surf rock, and their dynamic songwriting, which combined slow verses with raging refrains. While they grew a large European following, they were ignored by the U.S. mainstream, but nevertheless inspired a new generation of musicians, including Kurt Cobain.

BACKGROUND

The group met at the University of Massachusetts Amherst, where Joey Santiago and Black Francis were roommates.

6

albums... but a big influence on rock!

"PIXIES"

Joey Santiago spoke English as a second language and saw the word 'pixies' in the dictionary. He liked how it looked and its definition of 'mischievous little elves' and it was definitively adopted by the group in 1986.

TWISTED BIBLE

Black Francis's lyrics dwelled on dark themes, and were often inspired by violent stories from the Bible. He said "It's all those characters in the Old Testament. I'm obsessed with them. Why it comes out so much I don't know."

32

MUSICAL STYLE
Alternative rock

KEY DATES
Group began
in 1986

THE VOICE
Charles Michael Kittridge
Thompson IV – known on
stage as Black Francis –
had 'a hackle-raising
caterwaul'!

A BASSIST
Kim Deal joined
the group in response
to an ad placed
in the *Boston Phoenix*.

**LASTING
LEGACY**

Nirvana, Radiohead,
the Strokes, Bush,
Blur and Weezer
were all inspired
by the group.

A dark vision

Nirvana

Nirvana are synonymous with grunge. Combining distorted electric guitars with fatalistic, angst-filled lyrics, the group hailed the resurgence of punk rock and heavy metal in the 1990s. Formed in Seattle in 1987, they hit the big time with their album *Nevermind*. Powered by Krist Novoselic on bass and Dave Grohl on drums, frontman and guitarist Kurt Cobain became revered for his dramatic vocals, delivering quiet, forboding verses, followed by heavy, tortured choruses, leading him to become adopted by fans as the 'spokesman of a generation'.

LIFE AFTER NIRVANA

The group disbanded after the tragic death of Cobain in 1994. Grohl went on to found another influential band, the Foo Fighters, singing lead vocals and alternately playing drums and lead guitar. Novoselic became a sometime collaborator.

SELECTED DISCOGRAPHY

1991
Nevermind

1993
In Utero

1994
MTV Unplugged in New York

1996
From the Muddy Banks of the Wishkah (live)

INFLUENCE

Kurt Cobain was a big fan of the Beatles and even covered one of their songs 'And I Love Her'.

SMELLS LIKE TEEN SPIRIT

At a party, Kathleen Hanna, singer with Bikini Kill, scrawled 'Kurt smells like Teen Spirit' on a wall. Kurt Cobain adopted the phrase, using it in one of their best-known songs... only later discovering that 'Teen Spirit' was a deodorant!

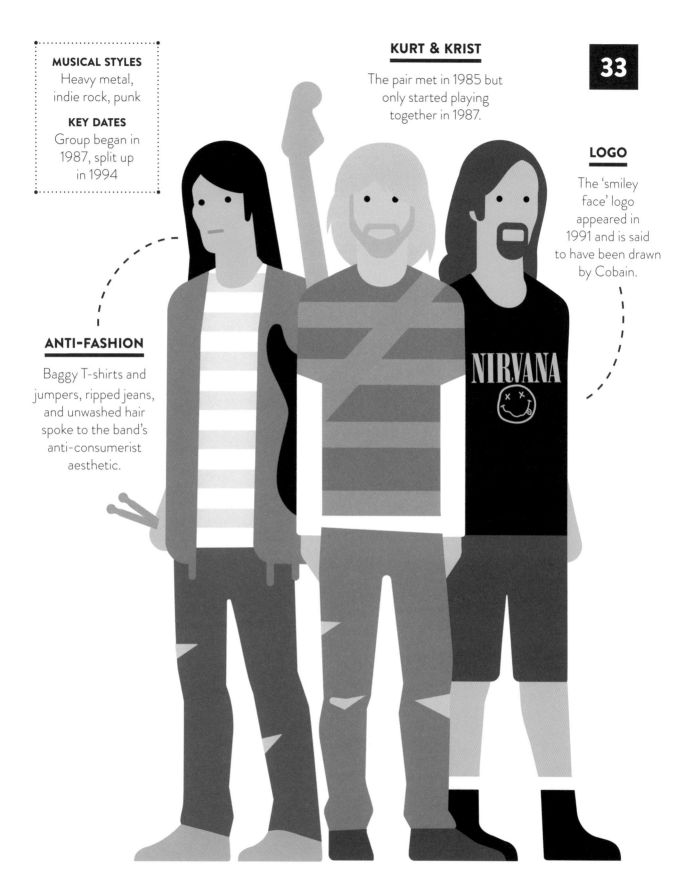

33

MUSICAL STYLES
Heavy metal, indie rock, punk

KEY DATES
Group began in 1987, split up in 1994

KURT & KRIST
The pair met in 1985 but only started playing together in 1987.

LOGO
The 'smiley face' logo appeared in 1991 and is said to have been drawn by Cobain.

ANTI-FASHION
Baggy T-shirts and jumpers, ripped jeans, and unwashed hair spoke to the band's anti-consumerist aesthetic.

NIRVANA

Smells Like Teen Spirit

Blur

London-based band Blur took inspiration from British bands of the 1960s and '70s, including the Jam, the Kinks and the Beatles, and reimagined their sound to create a fresh, unique brand of pop which helped to define a new era of music in the UK: Britpop. The media made much of their race to the top of the charts against their northern rivals, Manchester-based band Oasis, although in reality, the animosity between the bands was overhyped, and perhaps distracted people from the fact that Blur was, and still are, a great group.

5 DATES

1988
Began in Colchester (Essex)

1991
Leisure

1994
Parklife:
a hit with the public

2003
Think Tank:
the group takes a break

2015
The Magic Whip: it comes back

ACTIVISM

Damon Albarn continues to be involved in charity work, in particular for Oxfam, a charity working against injustice and poverty.

CONCERT

After a seven year gap, Blur played Glastonbury in 2009, getting rave reviews as 'the best Glastonbury headliners in an age' and later performed a huge gig at Hyde Park.

BRITPOP

Britpop was a British rock movement which appeared in the middle of the 1990s and witnessed the emergence of groups like Supergrass, Oasis, Blur and Suede. This bright, catchy pop music was an antidote to the U.S.-led grunge being made at the time.

MULTI-TALENTED

Damon Albarn, the lead singer of Blur, later co-founded Gorillaz, Monkey: Journey to the West, and the Good, the Bad & the Queen – which shows his musical diversity and great creativity. He also became a champion of world music.

34

MUSICAL STYLE
Britpop,
alternative rock

KEY DATES
Group was
founded in 1988

AT THE HELM
... Damon Albarn –
composer
and founder
of the group.

MODS #2
Blur's style was
inspired by the mod
look of the 1960s.

THE NAME
Damon Albarn,
Graham Coxon, Alex
James and Dave
Rowntree formed Blur.
They were originally
called Seymour.

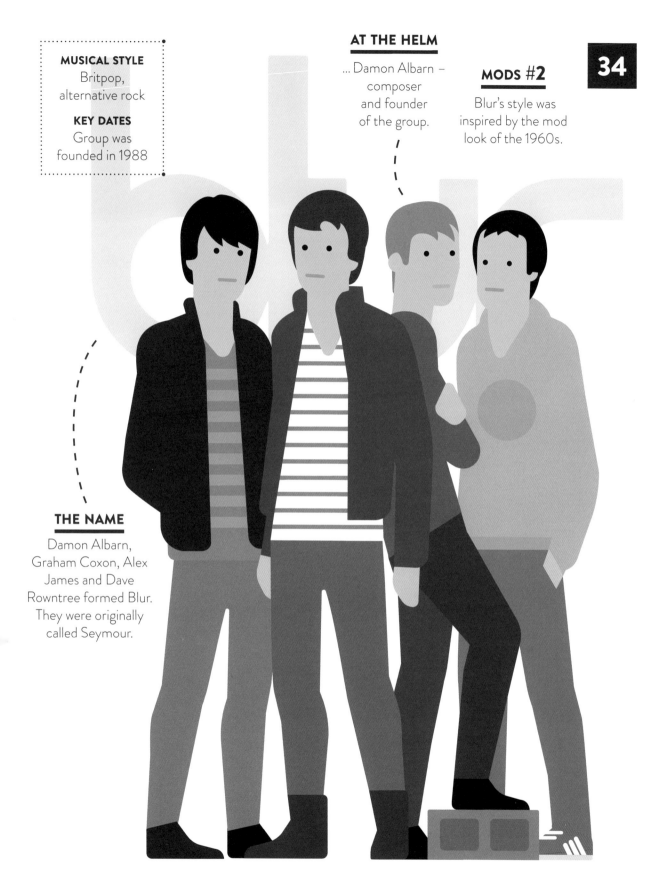

Britpop!

Radiohead

One of the most inventive groups of their generation, Radiohead had a long road to success. Forming at school in 1985, it wasn't until the band released their single 'Creep' in 1992 that they began to be noticed. Two decade-defining albums – *The Bends* and *OK Computer* – followed, propelling Radiohead to a new level of international success. Summing up the reason for their success, singer Thom Yorke said, "What really blew my head off was the fact that people got [...] all the textures and the sounds and the atmospheres we were trying to create."

GOING SOLO

Thom Yorke balances Radiohead with other projects including Atoms for Peace, which includes Red Hot Chili Peppers bassist Flea and Radiohead producer Nigel Godrich. Meanwhile, drummer Phil Selway has a solo career, while Jonny Greenwood scores music for films.

SELECTED DISCOGRAPHY

1995
The Bends

1997
OK Computer

2000
Kid A

2003
Hail to the Thief

2016
A Moon Shaped Pool

Over **30** million albums sold worldwide!

INTERNET REVOLUTION

Revolutionary not just in their music making, but also in their approach to selling and distributing it, Radiohead's album *In Rainbows* was released through the band's website as pay-what-you-want download! The move made headlines around the world.

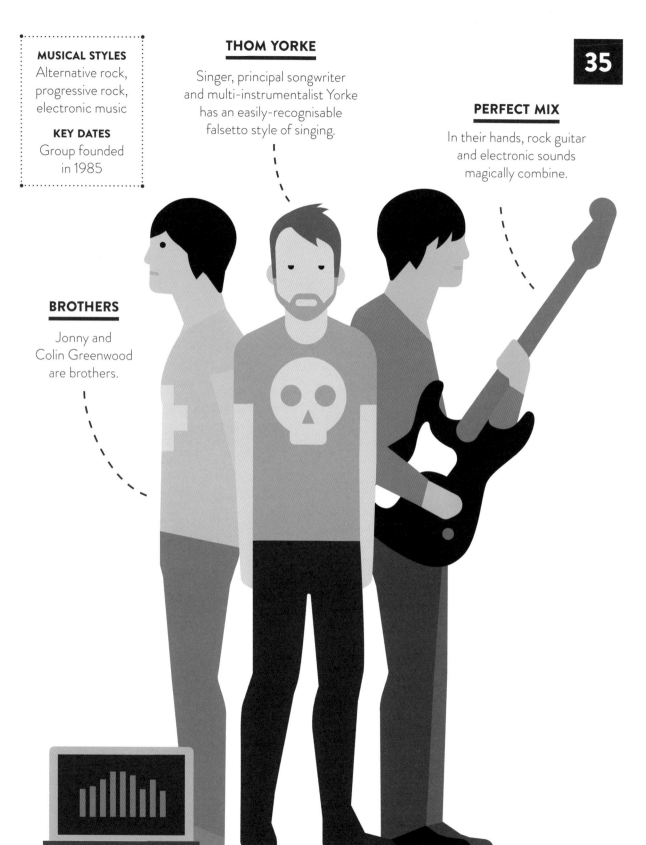

35

MUSICAL STYLES
Alternative rock, progressive rock, electronic music

KEY DATES
Group founded in 1985

THOM YORKE
Singer, principal songwriter and multi-instrumentalist Yorke has an easily-recognisable falsetto style of singing.

PERFECT MIX
In their hands, rock guitar and electronic sounds magically combine.

BROTHERS
Jonny and Colin Greenwood are brothers.

Art rock

Wu-Tang Clan

American hip-hop group the Wu-Tang Clan came to fame at the beginning of the 1990s when they released their debut album, *Enter the Wu-Tang (36 Chambers)*, which is widely recognised as one of the best hip-hop albums of all time. Influenced by martial arts cinema, the Wu-Tang Clan's sound samples the underground soul of the 1960s and 1970s, and is violent, urban, minimalist and very dark, while their lyrics are full of their native New York slang and are often delivered in a threatening, urgent rap style.

BACKGROUND

Assembled in the early 1990s by de facto leader RZA, the group hails from Staten Island, in New York.

WU-TANG KILLA BEEZ

The Wu-Tang Clan has helped to launch the career of an ever-growing list of rappers, singers and producers, who became known as known as Killa Beez or Wu Fam. The members of the group themselves also each have solo careers.

SINGLE COPY

In 2015, the group brought out a new album called *Once Upon a Time in Shaolin*, but only a single copy was made, which was sold to a rich entrepreneur for two million dollars ! It had taken six years to make.

EXPERIMENTATION

The Wu-Tang Clan consists of nine singers who forged a distinctive style of rapping at incredible speed, and who have inspired modern-day artists including Kanye West and Just Blaze.

36

MUSICAL STYLES
Hip-hop,
East Coast rap

KEY DATES
Group began
in 1992

POWER BEHIND
THE THRONE

Producer RZA
is considered
the leader of the group.

THE CLAN

Wu-Tang set themselves up as
a collective, a brotherhood
of rappers.

THE LOGO

A W, but also a bat, the logo was devised by
the graffiti artist Allah Mathematics.

Enter the Wu-Tang

Daft Punk

MAJOR ALBUM

In its first week, their album *Random Access Memories* sold more than a million copies!

Emerging out of the French house scene of the late 1990s, Daft Punk experimented with drum machines and synthesisers to create a unique sound that combined elements of electronic, house and techno music. Initially, the duo achieved only niche recognition, but later broadened their audience thanks to hits such as 'Around the World' and 'One More Time', which made electronica more melodic and commercial. But the Frenchmen are perhaps best known for donning robot costumes onstage... and maintaining a mysterious silence offstage!

EXPLOSIVE MIX

They explain their personas thus: "We did not choose to become robots. There was an accident in our studio. We were working on our sampler, and at exactly 9:09 a.m. on September 9, 1999, it exploded. When we regained consciousness, we discovered that we had become robots."

SELECTED DISCOGRAPHY

1997
Homework

2001
Discovery

2005
Human After All

2010
Tron: Legacy

2013
Random Access Memories

STARBOYS

Guy-Manuel de Homem-Christo and Thomas Bangalter initially started out making indie music with the short-lived group Darlin', before setting up Daft Punk on their own, and switching their acoustic instruments for electronic ones.

EXPERIMENTATION

The duo combined talents with Joseph Trapanese to score the soundtrack for the film *Tron: Legacy*, in which they had cameo roles, wearing their trademark helmets.

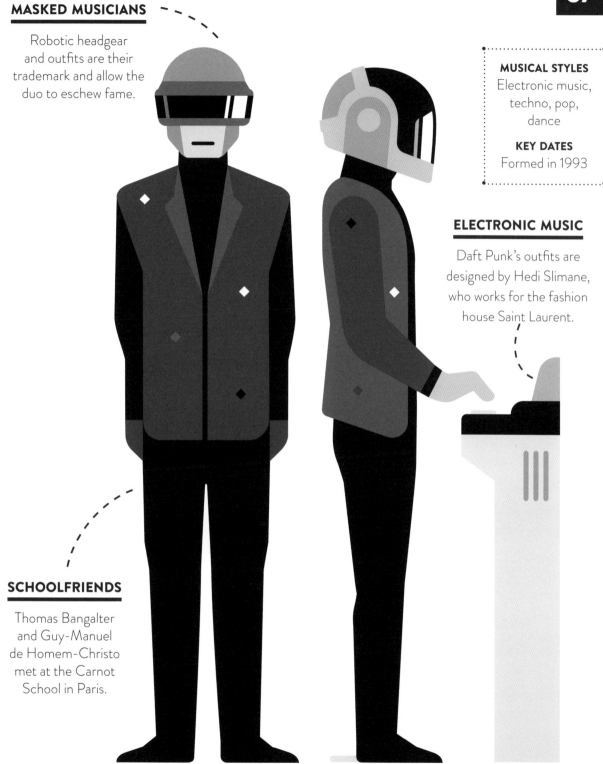

37

MASKED MUSICIANS

Robotic headgear and outfits are their trademark and allow the duo to eschew fame.

MUSICAL STYLES
Electronic music, techno, pop, dance

KEY DATES
Formed in 1993

ELECTRONIC MUSIC

Daft Punk's outfits are designed by Hedi Slimane, who works for the fashion house Saint Laurent.

SCHOOLFRIENDS

Thomas Bangalter and Guy-Manuel de Homem-Christo met at the Carnot School in Paris.

French house robots

The White Stripes

American rock duo the White Stripes sent up an angry missile of sound during the dying days of rock towards the end of the 1990s. Leading the revival of garage rock, their music, which melded blues with thundering garage and heavy rock, was easily distinguished by its implacable rhythms and raw simplicity. The pair were equally identifiable, dressing themselves – and all their album covers – in a palette solely of red, white and black, and their hits, including stadium anthem 'Seven Nation Army', re-established rock as a credible genre... and not before time!

BACKGROUND

The band was formed in 1997 in Detroit, Michigan, in 1997, where an underground hard-core punk scene known as Midwest hard-core emerged and later swept America in the early 1980s.

EXPERIMENTATION

Jack White is a team player. He produces numerous artists, has already played in five groups including Dead Weather and the Raconteurs and he's not finished yet!

5 DATES

1999
White Stripes

2003
Elephant

2007
Icky Thump

2010
Under Great White Northern Lights (live)

2012
Blunderbuss, Jack White's 1ˢᵗ solo album

JUMP IN TIME

Jack Gillis met Meg White as a senior at high school, and the pair went on to marry, Jack taking Meg's name, contrary to tradition. Jack started out playing with other bands, but formed the White Stripes with Meg when she learned to play the drums.

WORK ETHIC

Jack explained how they came to be named after stripy sweets, saying "Meg loves peppermints, and we were going to call ourselves the Peppermints. But since our last name was White, we decided to call it 'the White Stripes'".

38

MUSICAL STYLES
Garage, punk, blues, rock

KEY DATES
Formed in 1997, broke up in 2011

PRIVATE LIFE
To keep the focus on their music, Jack spread a story that the pair were brother and sister, despite the fact that they had been married, then divorced.

FRONTMAN
Jack White was on vocals and played a red and white fibreglass Res-o-Glas Airline guitar.

ON THE BEAT
Meg White played drums and sang.

The revenge of the guitar

Beyoncé

Blessed with a powerful, velvety voice dubbed 'one of the most compelling instruments in popular music', Beyoncé Knowles first made a name for herself as part of R&B girl group Destiny's Child before launching her solo career, which saw her become one of the best-selling music artists in history. Growing up in Houston, Texas, she began singing and dancing as a child and went on to dominate the charts with her brand of empowering pop and R&B, cleverly managing her fame to indulge her passions for film, fashion and feminism.

POWER COUPLE

Aged 18, Beyoncé met Shawn 'Jay-Z' Carter, a rapper and businessman, who has sold more than 100 million records himself. They later went on to marry, forming one of the most influential power couples the music industry has ever seen.

5 DATES

1981
Born in Houston, Texas

1997-2001
Career with Destiny's Child

2003
First solo album, *Dangerously in Love*

2008
Marriage with Jay-Z

2012
First child, Blue Ivy

CONCERT

In 2013, her half-time performance at the Super Bowl, became the second most watched interval of all time.

FIERCE FEMALE

Her two hits 'Crazy in Love' and 'Single Ladies (Put a Ring on It)', allowed Beyoncé to lay claim to not one, but two of the greatest singles of the naughties. To sing with sass, she adopted an aggressive onstage alter ego, who she called Sasha Fierce.

39

THE VOICE

She has a range of three octaves and has great breath control, power and rhythm.

MUSICAL STYLE
R&B

KEY DATES
Born in 1981

MOVES

As a dancer and choreographer, Beyoncé has performed some of the most iconic routines from 21st century pop.

WHO RUNS THE WORLD?

Beyoncé's career – and her songs – prove her to be (in her own words) 'a modern-day feminist'.

Queen of R&B

Arcade Fire

Canadian indie rock band Arcade Fire are the genuine article. Their thoughtful, uplifting anthems make use of a host of unconventional instruments, including the horn, harp and hurdy-gurdy, setting them apart from mainstream pop, but winning them a huge global audience, with the likes of Bono, the Rolling Stones and even Barack Obama singing their praises! Down to earth and unassuming, the band are known for adventuring off the beaten track to play for audiences in places like Haiti and Jamaica, explore other cultures and take part in humanitarian work.

ACTIVISM

The group have used their fame to support a number of good causes, and went to help those who had survived the earthquake in Haiti.

INFLUENCE

Listen to their music and you can hear the impact of the legends that have gone before them, like the Beatles, David Bowie, the Cure, New Order, and Radiohead.

A DIFFICULT START

At the start of their career, the band struggled to get backing from a major record label. It was the release of their EP in 2003 – plus the excited buzz around their live performances – that helped them to secure their fame.

LIKE AN ORCHESTRA

Cult director Spike Jonze helped to establish the band as international stars when he directed the video to their title track 'The Suburbs'. He later used their music in his Hollywood movies *Her* and *Where the Wild Things Are*.

5 DATES

2001
Formed in Montréal

2004
Funeral

2007
Neon Bible

2010
The Suburbs

2013
Reflektor

MUSICAL STYLES
Indie rock, lyric pop

KEY DATES
Group began in 2001

POWER COUPLE

Régine Chassagne and Win Butler met at university and later married.

MULTI-INSTRUMENTALISTS

The band uses a vast array of different instruments, often switching instruments onstage.

COUNTRY

The band is based in Montreal – and most of its members are Canadian.

The fire of Montreal

Chronology

1954

'Rock Around the Clock' by **Bill Haley**.
Rock 'n' roll hits the whole world.

———

Elvis Presley records his first hit,
'That's All Right (Mama)'.

1962

The **Rolling Stones'** first concert at the
Marquee Jazz Club in London.

———

The **Beatles** record their first single,
'Love Me Do'.

1971

'Stairway to Heaven' by **Led Zeppelin**
announces the coming of hard rock.

———

L.A. Woman by **the Doors** is released.

1976

Punk lights up England. **Sex Pistols** are the
standard-bearers for the phenomenon.

———

The song 'Dancing Queen'
by **ABBA** is a worldwide hit.

1991

Nevermind by **Nirvana** triumphs,
reviving punk rock via grunge.

Niggaz4Life by **N.W.A** comes out.

1993

Dr Dre (ex-**N.W.A**) popularises
gangsta rap with
'Nuthin' but a G Thang'.

1965

The **Who** sing 'My Generation'.

———

The **Stones** sing '(I Can't Get No) Satisfaction'.

———

As for **Bob Dylan**, he causes controversy when he plays an electric guitar at the Newport Folk Festival.

1967

First album by the **Velvet Underground**, illustrated with Andy Warhol's infamous yellow banana.

———

Are You Experienced by **The Jimi Hendrix Experience**. Guitar and sound revolution.

1979

Punk matures with *London Calling* by the **Clash**.

———

Massive pop/disco success for **Blondie** with *Heart of Glass*.

1982

Michael Jackson's *Thriller*, with accompanying video, is released. Revolution on MTV.

———

The Cure releases the album *Pornography*.

1997

Radiohead release *OK Computer*, and go from being a small indie group to rock superstars.

———

Homework by **Daft Punk** is released.

2003

First solo album for **Beyoncé** : *Dangerously in Love*.

———

Elephant by **White Stripes** is released.

Inspiring | Educating | Creating | Entertaining

Brimming with creative inspiration, how-to projects, and useful information to enrich your everyday life, Quarto Knows is a favourite destination for those pursuing their interests and passions. Visit our site and dig deeper with our books into your area of interest: Quarto Creates, Quarto Cooks, Quarto Homes, Quarto Lives, Quarto Drives, Quarto Explores, Quarto Gifts, or Quarto Kids.

Music Legends © 2017 Gallimard Jeunesse, Paris
Translation © 2018 Quarto Publishing plc.

First Published in 2017 in French by Gallimard Jeunesse, France.
First Published in 2018 in English by Wide Eyed Editions, an imprint of
The Quarto Group
The Old Brewery, 6 Blundell Street, London N7 9BH, United Kingdom.
T (0)20 7700 6700 F (0)20 7700 8066 **www.QuartoKnows.com**

A catalogue record for this book is available from the British Library.

ISBN 978-1-78603-149-5

The illustrations were created digitally
Set in Brandon Grotesque and Gotham Rounded

Manufactured in Guangdong, China CC0518

9 8 7 6 5 4 3 2 1

MIX
Paper from
responsible sources
FSC® C008047

Collect the rest in the series!

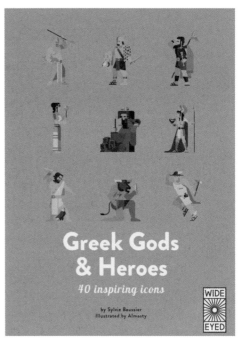

Greek Gods & Heroes
978-1-78603-147-1

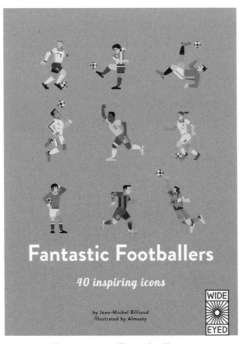

Fantastic Footballers
978-1-78603-146-4

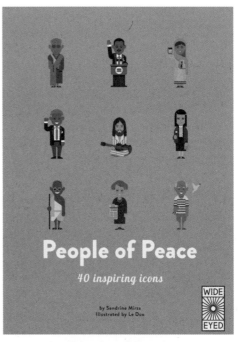

People of Peace
978-1-78603-148-8